# CREATING MEANING

## Advanced Reading and Writing

Laurie Blass

Hannah Friesen

Kathy Block

**OXFORD**

UNIVERSITY PRESS

**OXFORD**
UNIVERSITY PRESS

198 Madison Avenue
New York, NY 10016 USA

Great Clarendon Street, Oxford OX2 6DP UK

Oxford University Press is a department of the University of Oxford.
It furthers the University's objective of excellence in research, scholarship,
and education by publishing worldwide in

Oxford  New York

Auckland  Cape Town  Dar es Salaam  Hong Kong  Karachi
Kuala Lumpur  Madrid  Melbourne  Mexico City  Nairobi
New Delhi  Shanghai  Taipei  Toronto

With offices in

Argentina  Austria  Brazil  Chile  Czech Republic  France  Greece
Guatemala  Hungary  Italy  Japan  Poland  Portugal  Singapore
South Korea  Switzerland  Thailand  Turkey  Ukraine  Vietnam

OXFORD and OXFORD ENGLISH are registered trademarks of
Oxford University Press

© Oxford University Press 2008

Original edition published by and © Oxford University Press, 70 Wynford
Drive, Don Mills, Ontario, Canada.

Database right Oxford University Press (maker)

Editorial Director: Sally Yagan
Senior Managing Editor: Patricia O'Neill
Design Director: Robert Carangelo
Design Manager: Maj-Britt Hagsted
Senior Designer: Michael Steinhofer
Image Editor: Robin Fadool
Cover Design: Stacy Merlin
Project Leader, ADP: Bridget McGoldrick
Manufacturing Manager: Shanta Persaud
Manufacturing Controller: Eve Wong

ISBN: 978 0 19 472300 8

Printed in Hong Kong.

10 9 8 7 6 5 4 3

ACKNOWLEDGMENTS

*Realia by:* Amelia Janes, Earth Illustrated Inc.: p. 113

*We would like to thank the following for their permission to reproduce photographs:*
Cover: Place Furstenberg, Paris, August 7, 8, 9, 1985 #1 by David Hockney.

*Interior:* age footstock: 45; CBS: This image serviced Tuesday, July 31, 2007.
Copyright CBS Broadcasting Inc. All Rights Reserved. 29; Corbis: 97, 107;
Corbis: Rob Lewine 1, Tom & Dee Ann McCarthy 18, Edimédia 37, Philip
Wallick 53, moodboard 145; Index Stock 67; ImageState RM Rights Managed
Photograph 36; JupiterImages Corporation 11; Photo Researchers, Inc.:
John Cole 121; Stock Connection 75; SuperStock, Inc. 27; Downloaded from
http://www.en.wikipedia.org/wiki/Image:BetaStirlingTG4web.jpg Rombic
Drive Beta Type Stirling Design – Screenshot von meinem eignen Design.
Fehlt der Regenerator u. A: 29

*The publisher would like to acknowledge these valuable sources of information
incorporated in the articles of this textbook:*

p. 4: Family definition from The Vanier Institute of the Family, www.
vifamily.ca/about/about.html. pp. 11–12: Yvonne Block. pp. 18–19: "Few
Holidays for These Dads" by Tony Hicks. *Contra Costa Times,* June 18,
2006. Used by permission. pp. 29–30: "Segway Creator Unveils His Next
Act," by Erick Shonfeld. www.cnnmoney.com, Jan. 16, 2006. pp. 36–38:
"About Impressionism," from *Impressionism: Paintings Collected by European
Museums,* A Resource Packet for Educators. pp. 45–46: Source: *Creating
Meaning* (Canadian edition). pp. 55–57: "Global Warming Fast Facts,"
by Brian Handwerk. December 6, 2004. National Geographic News,
NationalGeogrpahic.com. pp. 61–63: "Disaster reduction and the human
cost of disaster." © 2005, the humanitarian news and analysis service, IRIN.
www.irinnews.org/webspecials/DR/default.asp. Used by permission. pp.
67–68: "Funnel Fury" by Dane Lanken. Originally appeared in *Canadian
Geographic,* July/August 1996. Copyright © 1996 by Dane Lanken. Reprinted
and adapted with permission. pp. 76–77: Source: "Road to sanctuary: the
process can be arduous for many asylum seekers," by Sarah Karp. *The Chicago
Reporter,* April 2005. www.thechicagoreporter.com. pp. 81–83: "A Fable for
Our Time" by Barb Toews from *Conciliation Quarterly,* Vol. 15, no. 3. Summer
1996. © Mennonite Conciliation Service, Akron, PA. pp. 86–87: Copyright
© 1997 by *The New York Times Company.* pp. 99–100: *Training for the Cross-
Cultural Mind: A Handbook for Cross-Cultural Trainers and Consultants,* Second
Edition, by Pierre Casse. SIETAR. The Society for Intercultural Education,
Training and Research, USA. Used with permission. pp. 107–108: *Dancing
with a Ghost: Exploring Indian Reality* by Rupert Ross. Elsevier. pp. 113–114:
"Expats in India", by Sabith Khan. Reprinted with permission from Little
India (www.littleindia.com). http://www.littleindia.com/february2005/
ExpatsinIndia.htm. p. 123: Written by Dr. Sheryl Bergmann Drewe, the
University of Manitoba. Reference: Simon, R. (1991). *Fair Play: Sports, Values
& Society.* Boulder Col.: Westview Press. pp. 129–130: "Family Presences
during CPR and Invasive procedures," Karen L. Spittler. Pulmonary Reviews.
com. http://www.pulmonaryreviews.com/mar06/family.html. pp. 135–136:
"Medical Ethics: A Ghastly Way to Practice" by Charlene Sadler. Originally
appeared in *The Globe and Mail,* 6 June 1998. With updates from: "Learning to
cut on virtual cadavers," by Michael Hill, 22 October 2006. *theglobeandmail.
com.* p. 148: "The Baby Boom" from *Boom, Bust & Echo* by David K. Foot
with Daniel Stoffman. Publ.: Macfarlane Walter & Ross, © 1996, Toronto,
Canada. pp. 18–20. pp. 153–154: "Generation Me" by Jean M. Twenge. http://
www.generationme.org/excerpt.html. © 2006 Jean M. Twenge. Used by
permission. pp. 155–156: "Generation Me: Why Today's Young Americans
Are More Confident, Assertive, Entitled—and More Miserable—Than
Ever Before" Reviewed by Aaron Shulman, www.aarpmagazine.org,
January 2006. pp. 161–162: "Generation Y: The New Global Citizens" from
http://www.merrillassociates.net/topic/2004/06/generation-y-the-new-
global-citizens/ Created and maintained by Merrill Associates. Copyright
1996-2006. Used by permission. pp. 172–173: Lenhart, Amanda, Madden,
Mary. "Social Networking Websites and Teens: An Overview." Pew Internet
& American Life Project, January 3, 2007, http://www.pewinternet.org/pdfs/
PIP_SNS_Data_Memo_Jan_2007.pdf, accessed on August 15, 2007. Used by
permission. pp. 174–175: "Web of Risks: Students adore social-networking
sites like Facebook, but indiscreet postings can mean really big trouble."
by Brad Stone. *Newsweek,* August 21, 2006. pp. 180–183: "A privacy paradox:
Social networking in the United States," by Susan B. Barnes. *First Monday* vol.
11, number 9 (September 2006). http://firstmonday.org/issues/issue11_9/
barnes/index.html. Used by permission. pp. 193–194: "Experts Discuss
MySpace Issues" by Sarah H. Wright. This article originally appeared on the
MIT News Office website, May 24, 2006. Used by permission.

# CREATING MEANING
## Advanced Reading and Writing

# Contents

To the Teacher | vii

| | TITLE | PAGE |
|---|---|---|
| **Chapter 1** | **Relationships: A New Definition of the Family** | **1** |
| | Changing the Definition | 3 |
| | James | 11 |
| | Mr. Mom | 18 |
| **Chapter 2** | **Innovators: People Who Make a Difference** | **27** |
| | Innovations for the Developing World | 29 |
| | Finding a New Way to Paint | 36 |
| | Frank Gehry | 45 |
| **Chapter 3** | **Natural Disasters** | **53** |
| | Global Warming | 55 |
| | Disaster Reduction | 61 |
| | Funnel Fury | 67 |
| **Chapter 4** | **Roads to Justice** | **75** |
| | The Road to Sanctuary | 76 |
| | Victim Offender Reconciliation—A New Approach to Justice | 81 |
| | Alternative Sentencing | 86 |
| **Chapter 5** | **Crossing Cultures** | **97** |
| | Culture Shock | 99 |
| | Seeing Through the Rules | 107 |
| | Expatriates in India | 113 |
| **Chapter 6** | **Ethical and Social Issues** | **121** |
| | Fair Play | 123 |
| | Being There | 129 |
| | Medical Ethics: A Ghastly Way to Practice | 135 |
| **Chapter 7** | **Generations** | **145** |
| | The Baby Boom | 148 |
| | Generation Me | 153 |
| | The New Global Citizens | 161 |
| **Chapter 8** | **Life Online: The Impact of Social Networks** | **169** |
| | Social Networking Sites and Teens | 172 |
| | A Privacy Paradox | 180 |
| | Discussion: MySpace and DOPA | 193 |
| | Appendix | 201 |
| | Vocabulary Index | 202 |

| READING SKILL | CRITICAL ANALYSIS | VOCABULARY | WRITING |
|---|---|---|---|
| Pre-reading: previewing; predicting | Distinguishing fact from opinion | Identifying signal words | Sentence types; summarizing |
| Identifying main ideas and supporting information | Analyzing and ranking significance | Identifying and using synonyms | Organizing ideas; writing an essay |
| Scanning for information; chronological order | Analyzing causes and effects | Identifying suffixes and prefixes | Thesis statements; describing a process |
| Using a graphic organizer to make comparisons | Identifying point of view | Identifying and using collocations | Paraphrasing; writing comparison essays |
| Taking notes on a reading; understanding proverbs; recognizing organizational patterns: cause/effect | Using empathy | Identifying positive and negative connotations | Recognizing different writing styles; Writing cause/effect essays |
| Analyzing the structure of an argument; mapping information | Evaluating costs and benefits | Skipping unknown words | Writing argumentative essays |
| Identifying mixed organizational patterns | Recognizing stereotypes | Understanding idioms in context | Writing a critique |
| Taking notes for a research paper; analyzing a problem-solution passage | Synthesizing information | Recognizing and using lead-in expressions | Writing a research paper; documenting sources |

# To the Teacher

Welcome to *Creating Meaning*, an advanced reading and writing text that prepares students for the reading, writing, and critical thinking skills required in an academic environment.

In academic settings, students must work with large amounts of information presented in written form. They must be able to comprehend ideas, select and synthesize relevant information, and communicate accurately and analytically in their own writing. In other words, for academic success, students need to be actively involved in the construction of meaning in both reading and writing. *Creating Meaning* is designed to provide students with ample opportunities to practice these important skills.

## Features

*Creating Meaning* includes a variety of authentic readings, writing tasks, and stimulating critical thinking and discussion activities that provide students with opportunities for synthesizing and communicating information by means of traditional academic rhetorical modes such as process, comparison, cause/effect, and argument.

In addition, extensive practice with essential academic skills such as paraphrasing, summarizing, and documenting sources culminate in writing a research paper with multiple citations.

The authentic passages in Creating Meaning reflect academic disciplines such as sociology, anthropology, law, and physical science. Engaging topics on contemporary issues such as Internet privacy and "Generation Me" provide opportunities for selecting and synthesizing the information required for the writing tasks. Text types are informal and formal, ranging from personal accounts to academic journal articles and extend from 7.2 to 12.0 on the Flesch-Kincaid readability scale.

Passages are accompanied by reading- and vocabulary-skill development activities such as previewing, note taking, and identifying signal words. Vocabulary activities reinforce key terms from the passages that appear in the Academic Word List (AWL).

In addition, many passages serve as rhetorical models, providing students with the opportunity to analyze a variety of specific organizational structures as a means of increasing their comprehension, their ability to remember information, and their ability to organize information in writing.

Finally, *Creating Meaning* has been designed so that writing tasks become increasingly complex as students progress through the text. For example, Chapter 1 briefly reviews summarizing, Chapter 2 presents the components of a well-organized paragraph, and Chapter 3 covers thesis statements. By Chapter 8, students are ready to tackle a research paper.

# Chapter Walk-Through

*Creating Meaning* chapters include four sections: **Reading 1**, **Reading 2**, **Reading 3**, and **Writing Focus**.

Each chapter begins with **Chapter Objectives**, a boxed list of the reading, critical analysis, vocabulary, and writing skills that alert students to what they will learn in that chapter.

**Reading 1** is the first of three reading sections in the chapter. Before students read, they work through a series of pre- and post-reading activities that scaffold the passage.

**Previewing** gives students an idea of what the passage is about by having them look at the organizing elements of the text such as the title and any headings, pictures, or captions that accompany it.

**Thinking about the Topic** is a series of small-group discussion questions related to the topic of the passage. They help students discover what they already know about the topic.

**Making Predictions** encourages students to predict the purpose and main ideas of the reading based on their previewing and discussion activities. As they read, they confirm their predictions, which helps them focus on and retain key facts.

**The reading passage** presents information on one aspect of the chapter theme. It can be assigned as an in-class activity or as homework.

**Comprehension Check** questions elicit short, written answers that draw out the main and supporting ideas of the passage and serve as a summary of the passage. This can be assigned as an in-class activity or as homework.

Boxed **Reading skill** presentations introduce strategies such as Using Graphic Organizers to Make Comparisons. These skills help students analyze, understand, and retain the information that they read. The presentation is followed by a practice activity that allows students to apply the strategy by working with the passage they've just read. It can be assigned as an in-class activity or as homework.

Reading strategies and accompanying activities can appear in any of the three reading sections.

Boxed **Critical Analysis** presentations introduce thinking skills such as Identifying Point of View. These skills help students go beyond the text in their thinking, discussing, and writing about the chapter topic. The presentation is followed by a small-group, in-class practice activity that allows students to apply the strategy to the passage they've just read or to an aspect of the chapter topic.

Critical analysis skills are usually presented in the Reading 1 section and students continue to practice them throughout the chapter.

Boxed **Vocabulary** skill presentations introduce strategies such as Identifying Collocations. These skills help students decode, retain, and use new vocabulary as they encounter it. The presentation is followed by a practice activity that allows students to apply the strategy to the passage they've just read. This can be assigned as an in-class activity or as homework.

Vocabulary strategies and accompanying activities can appear in any of the three reading sections.

**Vocabulary in Context** is an activity that helps students acquire and work with Academic Word List items that appear in the passage they've just read. Activity types include fill-in-the-blank, matching, and writing short answers. This can be assigned as an in-class activity or as homework.

Boxed **Writing skill** presentations introduce strategies such as Organizing Ideas. These skills help students better express themselves in their writing. The presentation is followed by an opportunity to apply the strategy in a short writing activity related to the chapter topic that also serves as preparation for the culminating writing assignment. This can be assigned as an in-class activity or as homework.

Writing strategies and accompanying activities can appear in any of the three reading sections.

**Reading 2** is the second reading section in the chapter. The passage presents information on another aspect of the chapter theme. It can be assigned as an in-class activity or as homework.

This section proceeds in a fashion similar to that of the Reading 1 section, above.

**Reading 3** is the third reading section in the chapter. The passage presents information on an additional aspect of the chapter theme. It can be assigned as an in-class activity or as homework.

This section proceeds in a fashion similar to that of the Reading 1 section, above.

The **Writing Focus** section presents the main rhetorical focus of the chapter, along with the writing assignment.

The section begins with a boxed presentation of the **rhetorical focus**, such as Writing Comparison Essays. These presentations explain and model the rhetorical focus that students will use in their writing assignment for the chapter. Practice opportunities that can include analyzing a model, organizing information, and/or writing short passages, help students understand and integrate the presentation material.

The **Writing Assignment** presents a selection of writing prompts related to the chapter topic. Students may choose their own topics or one may be assigned to the entire class. The writing assignment can be done as homework.

**Preparing to Write** is a set of step-by-step suggestions for students to follow as they plan and organize their essays. These suggestions model and help students integrate aspects of the pre-writing process such as generating ideas, developing a point of view, gathering information, and organizing ideas for writing. Depending on their level of proficiency, students can either work through these steps in class with peer and/or instructor input or do this as homework.

Each chapter concludes with **After You Write**, a set of evaluation questions that help guide students though the revision process. Depending on their level of proficiency, students can either work through these questions in class with peer and/or instructor input or do this as homework. The revision can be assigned as homework.

# Chapter 1

# Relationships:
## A New Definition of the Family

## Chapter Objectives

| | |
|---|---|
| **Reading:** | Pre-reading |
| **Critical Analysis:** | Distinguishing Fact from Opinion |
| **Vocabulary:** | Identifying Signal Words |
| **Writing:** | Sentence Types |
| | Summarizing |

# Reading 1

## 1   Previewing

**Preview the reading on pages 3 to 4. Look at the title. Then read the introduction and the last paragraph.**

## 2   Thinking about the Topic

**In small groups, discuss your answers to the following questions.**

1. Is your family the same size as your parents' or your grandparents' family? If not, what might be the reasons for the change in size?

2. In what ways is your family important to you? Give an example.

3. How are the families that you know changing?

## 3   Making Predictions

**In small groups, discuss your answers to the following questions.**

1. What do you think is the main idea of the reading below?

2. What details or examples might the author include to develop the main idea?

*Now read the text and answer the questions that follow.*

# Changing the Definition

The family is under stress. In the past few decades, the number of divorces has increased dramatically around the world. In many countries, fewer people are getting married, and there is an

5   increase in single-parent families. Nevertheless, optimists say that the family is merely changing as it has done for thousands of years.

According to the Vanier Institute of the Family, families have always altered in size,

10   structure, and patterns of functioning. Over the centuries, families have been in a constant state of adaptation to the natural environment as well as to current political, religious, and social conditions. However, there have been few

15   periods in history during which families have changed as much as they did in the second half of the twentieth century.

There are a number of reasons for the changes in the family:

20   • The extended family that was once common is now relatively rare. This is due to the fact that older people have greater financial security and tend not to

25   live with their grown children.

• People are becoming more mobile. For example, one in five people in the United States moves every year, and the average American moves 11

30   times in his or her lifetime. Nuclear families move from one community to another in search of economic opportunity, and grown children tend to leave the community in

35   which they grew up.

• Contraception gives women choices in the number and spacing of their children. Many women choose to work outside the home rather than

40   stay at home to raise their children, as was the custom in the past.

• Liberalized divorce laws affect the family in that men and women can choose to leave less than

45   satisfactory relationships. This has resulted in increased numbers of single-parent families.

According to the Vanier Institute, people say that family is important to them. However, what

50   people value in families is not the same as what they valued in the past. For example, studies show that today, many people believe that caring for one another is more important than having a marriage certificate.

55   Therefore, with so much change taking place at such a rapid pace, is it time to redefine "family"? According to a 1997 report, psychologists who studied textbooks for definitions of the family could not find a specific definition. Rather, the

60   psychologists found descriptions of families. They noticed that textbooks defined families through pictures and stories referring to family life. The texts showed families in many different ways; for example, families with both parents, families with

65   single parents, and couples without children.

The Vanier Institute of the Family believes that families should be defined by their function rather than who is in them. It asserts that we can no longer define families by who belongs to them

70   because they are all so different. However, we can define families by what they do, because most of them still perform the same tasks they have dealt with for generations. For example, the family is where most learning, education, and socialization

75   take place; furthermore, it is a source of emotional sustenance and support and a significant unit of both economic production and consumption.

Any complete definition of what constitutes a family and its functions must allow for diversity

80   and be culturally neutral. It must not rely on one national, historical, religious, or ethical set of assumptions. This is a matter of great importance in free and pluralistic societies.

The following is the Vanier Institute's functional definition of *family*:

> Any combination of two or more persons who are bound together over time by ties of mutual consent, birth, and/or adoption or placement and who, together, assume responsibilities for variant combinations of some of the following:
>
> - Physical maintenance and care of group members
> - Addition of new members through procreation or adoption
> - Socialization of children
> - Social control of members
> - Production, consumption, distribution of goods and services, and
> - Affective nurturance—love

Just as individual human beings both act within society and act upon it, so families can be thought of as simultaneously active and receptive agents within society. Families, the many forces at work on them, and their contribution to society are best understood as systems, the sum of many interacting parts. Moreover, families are open systems. Families are open to all kinds of social, political, economic, and natural influences. At the same time, families greatly influence their environment. For example, families in advanced industrial societies appear to have fewer children. In turn, smaller families result in many other changes in society such as empty schools, lower demand for big cars and apartments, and a smaller workforce. Those changes, in turn, may influence families.

## 4  Comprehension Check

**Write your answers to the following questions.**

1. List the ways in which families have changed in the last few decades.

   Political, religious and social conditions to adaptation to the natural environ[ment]

2. State four reasons for these changes.

   a) The extended family that was once common is now relatively rare

   b) People are becoming more mobile.

   c) Contraception gives women choices in the number and spacing of their children

   d) Liberalized divorces laws affect the family and that men and women can choise to leave less than satisfatory relationships.

3. According to the reading, is what people value in families now the same as what they valued 25 years ago? Explain your answer.

   Now people don't give the same value as 25 years ago. I think how the people pay more attention in the meaning of things, and less in the "correct process. Like a marriage certificate.

4. How was family defined in the past? Why is it necessary to come up with a new definition of *family*?

   In the past they don't use a definiton was more like a descriptions of familias, throght pictures and stories referring to the family life. It's necessory a new definition of family, because so much change taking place at such a rapid pace.
   * the families should be defined by their function rather than who is in them

5. In your own words, explain what *open systems* means.

The familees doesn't matter them composition are always exposed and influenced for the environment

6. According to the Vanier Institute of the Family, who is in a family? Write your explanation in your own words.

- "Two or more persons who are bound together over time by tres of mutual consent".
- People who stay together and share the same responsabilities.

7. According to the Vanier Institute of the Family's definition, what are the responsibilities of a family? State them in your own words. The first answer is supplied for you.

a. Takes care of its members
b. Addition of new members through procreation or adoption.
c. Socialization of children
d. Social control of member - lifestyle or options in life.
e. Production, consumption, distribution of goods.
f. Natures and loves its members

8. Using the information from questions 6 and 7, write a paragraph in which you describe in your own words the Vanier Institute's definition of a family.

They defined the family like a primary group, is a small and open system. Almost everybody lot a member of one, and that have benefits and responsabilities, whit the family and the society.

## 5 Critical Analysis: Distinguishing Fact from Opinion

Read the following statements and decide whether the information is a fact or an opinion. Check (✔) Fact or Opinion. Then write a brief explanation of your decision on the line. Discuss your answers with your classmates.

1. In many countries, fewer people are getting married, and there is an increase in single-parent families.

   ☒ a.  Fact          ☐ b.  Opinion

   ...................................................................................................................................

2. People are becoming more mobile.

   ☒ a.  Fact          ☐ b.  Opinion

   ...................................................................................................................................

3. Caring for one another is more important than having a marriage certificate.

   ☐ a.  Fact          ☒ b.  Opinion

   ...................................................................................................................................

4. Many people believe that caring for one another is more important than having a marriage certificate.

   ☒ a.  Fact          ☐ b.  Opinion

   ...................................................................................................................................

5. Families should be defined by their function rather than by who is in them.

   ☐ a.  Fact          ☒ b.  Opinion

   ...................................................................................................................................

**Vocabulary ⇒ *Identifying Signal Words***

The reading "Changing the Definition" contains signal words such as *nevertheless, for example,* and *however*. Signal words function as transitions; that is, they link one idea to another or one paragraph to another. Identifying signal words as you read helps you understand. Using them in your writing makes it clearer and easier to read.

The chart below gives you information about signal words that are useful in writing:

| Signal Words | Purpose |
|---|---|
| *for example, for instance, such as* | Introduce examples |
| *first, second, then, next* | Indicate order of ideas |
| *likewise, similarly, also, furthermore, moreover* | Add information |
| *however, nevertheless, despite, on the other hand* | Contrast information; show different information |
| *in summary, in brief, for these reasons, to sum up* | Summarize |
| *in conclusion, thus, therefore* | Conclude |

## 6 Identifying Signal Words

**Find the following sentences in "Changing the Definition." Discuss with a partner the purpose of each of the underlined signal words in relation to the ideas around it.**

1. Nevertheless, optimists say that the family is merely changing as it has done for thousands of years. (para. 1)

2. For example, one in five people in the United States moves every year, and the average American moves 11 times in his or her lifetime. (para. 5)

3. Therefore, with so much change taking place at such a rapid pace, is it time to redefine "family"? (para. 9)

4. However, we can define families by what they do, because most of them still perform the same tasks they have dealt with for generations. (para. 10)

5. Moreover, families are open systems. (para. 13)

## 7 Vocabulary in Context

**The following sentences are from the reading. For each underlined word, choose the closest meaning: *a, b,* or *c.***

1. Nevertheless, optimists say that the family is merely changing as it has done for thousands of years. (para. 1)

   a. however
   b. in addition
   c. in conclusion

2. According to the Vanier Institute of the Family, families have always <u>altered</u> in size, structure, and patterns of functioning. (para. 2)

   a. refused to change
   b. changed
   c. improved

3. This is due to the fact that older people have greater <u>financial</u> security and tend not to live with their grown children. (para. 4)

   a. economic
   b. physical
   c. psychological

4. <u>Liberalized</u> divorce laws affect the family in that men and women can choose to leave less than satisfactory relationships. (para. 7)

   a. narrow-minded
   b. open-minded
   c. foolish

5. The Vanier Institute of the Family believes that families should be defined by their <u>function</u> rather than who is in them. (para. 10)

   a. lifestyles
   b. number of individuals
   c. what they do

6. For example, the family is where most learning, education, and socialization take place; <u>furthermore</u>, it is a source of emotional sustenance and support and a significant unit of both economic production and consumption. (para. 10)

   a. therefore
   b. however
   c. in addition

7. Any complete definition of what constitutes a family and its functions must allow for <u>diversity</u> and be culturally neutral. It must not rely on one national, historical, religious, or ethical set of assumptions. (para. 11)

   a. confusion
   b. variety
   c. disagreement

8. [A family is] Any combination of two or more persons who ... assume responsibilities for variant combinations of some of the following: ...

• Production, consumption, <u>distribution</u> of goods and services, and ... (box)

   a. sharing
   b. taking away
   c. providing

# Writing ➡ *Sentence Types—Simple and Compound Sentences*

There are four basic sentence types: simple, compound, complex, and compound-complex. Knowing about and using different sentence types varies your writing and makes it more interesting. It also helps you edit and revise your work.

A **simple sentence** is an independent clause. It has a subject and a verb.

EXAMPLES:   People are becoming more mobile.
             subject  verb

            In the past few decades, the number of divorces has increased dramatically.
                                       subject                    verb

A **compound sentence** consists of two independent clauses (simple sentences) that have been joined by a coordinating conjunction or a semicolon.

**a.** Two independent clauses can be joined by a coordinating conjunction (*and, but, or, for, nor, so, yet*).

EXAMPLES:   For example, one in five people in the United States moves every year, <u>and</u> the average
                                    subject                                    verb

            American moves 11 times in his or her lifetime.
             subject    verb

            Being a single parent adds some extra pressure, <u>but</u> it also makes things less complicated.
             subject          verb                                subject    verb

            James and Yvonne have lived together for seven years, <u>so</u> they think of themselves as a
             subject         verb                                      subject  verb

            "real" family.

NOTE:   Two independent clauses joined by a coordinating conjunction are separated by commas.

| Relationship of clauses joined by coordinating conjunctions |
| --- |

Additional information ➡ *and*      Contrasting information ➡ *but*      An effect after a cause ➡ *so*

**b.** Two independent clauses can also be joined by a semicolon (;). This kind of compound sentence is possible only when the two independent clauses are closely related in meaning. If they are not closely related, they should be written as two simple sentences, each ending with a period.

EXAMPLES:   Older textbooks defined families by who was in them; they showed two-parent families, families with single parents, and couples without children.

            Jared and Lisa live with their grandmother; Ali is being raised by his father.

**c.** A compound sentence can consist of two independent clauses joined by a semicolon and an adverbial conjunction. Some common adverbial conjunctions are as follows:

*furthermore*                                    *however*
*moreover*                                       *nevertheless*  } Contrasting information
*also*          } Additional information
*next*                                           *consequently*
                                                 *therefore*     } An effect after a cause
                                                 *thus*

NOTE:   Adverbial conjunctions are followed by a comma with the exception of *next*.

EXAMPLES:   Many changes in family structure have taken place over the past few decades; <u>therefore</u>, it may be time for a new definition.
            The family has been under stress recently; <u>however</u>, according to sociologists, the family is merely changing.

## 8  Combining Sentences

Combine each pair of simple sentences (or independent clauses) to form compound sentences. Use coordinating conjunctions and adverbial conjunctions.

1. Jane isn't married. She has lived with her partner for more than ten years.

2. Rafael wanted to be a good father. He quit his job and started working from home.

3. The price of the house has been reduced. Apparently nobody wants to buy it.

4. No one in that family has the same interests. They all do different things on the weekends.

5. Japanese women are having their first child at a later age than they did in the past. The birth rate in Japan has declined slightly in the past few years.

6. More Americans are living together instead of getting married. The divorce rate is declining in the United States.

7. Many people think that the United States has a high divorce rate. The United Kingdom and Sweden both have higher divorce rates than the United States.

8. Liberalized divorce laws make it easy for people to leave unsatisfactory marriages. People are getting married later.

## 9  Using Compound Sentences

Rewrite your answer to item 8, page 5, using compound sentences.

# Reading 2

## 1  Previewing

Preview the reading on pages 11 to 12. Look at the title. Then read the introduction and the last paragraph. Study the picture.

## 2  Thinking about the Topic

In small groups, discuss your answers to the following questions.

1. Have you ever wished you could choose your parents or family?

2. Describe a time when you and your mother or father did something on your own.

3. What do you think life is like for a single parent?

## 3  Making Predictions

In small groups, discuss your answers to the following questions.

1. Who or what do you think the reading below will be about?

2. What details or examples might the author include to develop the main idea?

*Now read the text and answer the questions that follow.*

# James

James coming into my life has been the best thing that has ever happened to me. It has taught me so much and adds so much satisfaction to my life. Although being a parent is often a demanding and even sometimes terrifying job, I cannot imagine life without him anymore. I have come to believe that no matter who you are, who your child is, and how your child came into your life, all parents share the same challenges.

My son James is 11 years old now. I am his foster parent[1]. He has lived with me for seven years, so we seldom think of it as a foster-care relationship. I am his "real" mom and he is my "real" son. It is a permanent relationship and a permanent placement by Child and Family Services. We do not and have not for many years used the word *foster*. Somehow I think that word might make him (and me) feel that we do not quite have the relationship that other moms and sons have. He, and I, both feel secure in our relationship. We have the same needs that biological families have.

I am a single parent. This adds some extra pressure, but it also makes things less complicated in some ways. There is no negotiating with a partner about what is best for James, but on the other hand, James has only one parental role model and influence. It also means that when I am tired, there is no other adult to take over for me. Therefore, at times, James has to deal with me when what I really need is some space.

James is Native American; I am white. Maintaining his cultural awareness is important, and I believe that his culture should not be ignored or replaced just because it is not the same as mine. My approach has been to let him take the lead here. At certain ages he has been more interested in his culture than at other times. This preteen age is a time when kids focus more on what they have that is the same as what other kids have rather than what sets them apart. I expect that as he gets older, he will start asking more about it again.

I worry sometimes about how people view him and how, as he grows older, this will affect him. At this point, he seems oblivious to any prejudice because of his culture. However, I have seen how some storekeepers, for example, watch him a little more than other children. Though it does not happen often, it does happen, and as he grows older, he may start to notice this.

When James was younger, I took him to some powwows[2] and read him books written and illustrated by Native American writers and artists. At a certain age, he seemed to become uninterested. At this time, I make sure that he has books written by people of his culture and some more informational books about legends and traditions of "his people" as he calls them. He loves reading and is an excellent reader, so he takes in lots of information. What I could have done and should probably still do is learn more myself about his culture instead of just providing him with the information. Parenting is a constant learning experience.

James has some special needs. By the time he was four years old, he had moved from home to home at least sixteen times. My focus has been on giving him a predictable and stable home atmosphere. More than anything, I believe he needs to know that he is safe and that I am present—physically as much as emotionally. He has some difficulty establishing his own limits and usually feels better about himself when they are set out clearly. In order to succeed, he needs to know what the rules, boundaries, and limits are. Therefore, we keep quite a regular schedule—as I have often heard social workers say about children like James, "routine, routine, routine."

As a single parent working full-time, I know I often miss the small things, and they have become dear to me, especially recently. I miss day-to-day things like stopping to listen to him tell a story about something that happened at school or to tell me about a book he is reading or a dream he had. I do well with the big decisions—about what I think will be in his best interest, where we should live, what school would be best for him, and so on.

I believe that all parents set their priorities according to what they believe to be crucial. I know that more than in any other area of my life, I struggle with parenting. It seems to me that it is the most important role I have at this time. I often wonder about how I am doing, what I might be missing, and what I need to change or let go of as my boy grows older. In sum, like most parents, I learn as I go.

---

**1 foster parent:** a person other than a biological parent who takes responsibility for raising a child without adopting him or her
**2 powwows:** gatherings of Native Americans

## 4 Comprehension Check

**Write your answers to the following questions.**

**1.** Is this mother-son relationship positive? How do you know?

.................................................................................................

.................................................................................................

.................................................................................................

**2.** What is one advantage of being a single parent, according to the author? What is one disadvantage?

.................................................................................................

.................................................................................................

.................................................................................................

**3.** What does the author mean when she says, "My approach has been to let him take the lead here"? (para. 4)

.................................................................................................

.................................................................................................

.................................................................................................

**4.** Who are "his people"? (para. 6)

.................................................................................................

**5.** What does this mother do to ensure that James knows about his culture?

.................................................................................................

.................................................................................................

.................................................................................................

Why is this necessary?

..................................................................................................................................

..................................................................................................................................

..................................................................................................................................

6. What is James especially good at?

..................................................................................................................................

7. How do James and his mother fit the Vanier Institute's definition of a family? Respond to each of the points in the definition. The first one has been done for you.

   a. *She cares for him.*

   b. ...........................................................................................................................

   c. ...........................................................................................................................

   d. ...........................................................................................................................

   e. ...........................................................................................................................

   f. ...........................................................................................................................

8. In one paragraph, explain in your own words how James and his mother fit the Vanier Institute's definition of the family.

..................................................................................................................................

..................................................................................................................................

..................................................................................................................................

..................................................................................................................................

..................................................................................................................................

..................................................................................................................................

## 5 Critical Analysis: Distinguishing Fact from Opinion

**Read the following statements and decide whether the information is a fact or an opinion. Check (✔) Fact or Opinion. Then write a brief explanation of your decision on the line. Discuss your answers with your classmates.**

1. James coming into my life has been the best thing that has ever happened to me.

   ☐ a.  Fact          ☐ b.  Opinion

   ..............................................................................................................................

2. According to the Adoption and Foster Care Analysis and Reporting System Report, there were 532,000 children in the foster care system in the United States in 2002.

   ☐ a.  Fact          ☐ b.  Opinion

   ..............................................................................................................................

3. Single parents account for 27 percent of U.S. family households with children under 18.

☐ a. Fact    ☐ b. Opinion

4. The number of single mothers in the United States increased from 3 million to 10 million between 1970 and 2000.

☐ a. Fact    ☐ b. Opinion

5. All parents set their priorities according to what they believe to be crucial.

☐ a. Fact    ☐ b. Opinion

## 6 Identifying Signal Words

**Find the following sentences in "James." Discuss with a partner the purpose of each of the underlined signal words in relation to the ideas around them.**

1. There is no negotiating with a partner about what is best for James, but <u>on the other hand</u>, James has only one parental role model and influence. (para. 3)

2. At this point, he seems oblivious to any prejudice because of his culture. <u>However</u>, I have seen how some storekeepers, for example, watch him a little more than other children. (para. 5)

3. At this point, he seems oblivious to any prejudice because of his culture. However, I have seen how some storekeepers, <u>for example</u>, watch him a little more than other children. (para. 5)

4. In order to succeed, he needs to know what the rules, boundaries, and limits are. <u>Therefore</u>, we keep quite a regular schedule—as I have often heard social workers say about children like James, "routine, routine, routine." (para. 7)

5. I often wonder about how I am doing, what I might be missing, and what I need to change or let go of as my boy grows older. <u>In sum</u>, like most parents, I learn as I go. (para. 9)

## 7 Vocabulary in Context

Read the words and their definitions in the list below. Then choose the word that fits best in the sentences that follow.

| Words | Definitions |
|---|---|
| challenges (para. 1) | tests |
| partner (para. 3) | person with whom you live |
| maintaining (para. 4) | continuing; keeping |
| culture (para. 4) | customs and ideas of a particular group of people |
| stable (para. 7) | unchanging |
| focus (para. 7) | area of concentration |
| set ... priorities (para. 9) | decide what is most important |
| crucial (para. 9) | very important |

1. Yvonne expanded James's exposure to his ............................ by taking him to powwows and reading books to him.

2. My ............................ is on my children's education because many studies have shown that paying attention to school activities can make children better students.

3. Parenting without a partner can be stressful, so it is ............................ for single parents to have some time off.

4. ............................ a good relationship with your spouse's parents is essential; not staying on good terms with in-laws can cause a lot of problems.

5. Not everyone agrees on how best to raise a child, so it's helpful to have good negotiating skills when you parent with a spouse or a ............................ .

6. Parenting can present problems for anyone, and Yvonne experiences the same ............................ that any parent faces.

7. Since both my husband and I have jobs now, our finances have become more ............................ .

8. A child who spends too much time watching TV and not getting homework done will have to learn how to ............................ .

## Writing ⇒ *Sentence Types—Complex Sentences*

A **complex sentence** is made up of an independent clause (complete sentence) and one or more dependent (subordinate) clauses. A subordinate clause is introduced by a subordinate conjunction or relative pronoun and modifies the main clause or some element in it.

**EXAMPLES:** (*main, principle, or independent clause*)

Parents with partners often must negotiate child-rearing techniques,
<br>subject                  verb

(*dependent clause*) while single parents are free to raise their children the way they want.
<br>                              subject    verb

(*main, principle, or independent clause*)

It can be challenging to raise a child as a single parent
<br>subject  verb

(*dependent clause*) because there is no other adult to share the experience.
<br>                             subject verb

**Note:** An independent clause can stand alone as a complete sentence; however, a dependent clause by itself is a sentence fragment.

**EXAMPLES:** Single parents are free to raise their children the way they want.

*complete sentence*

While single parents are free to raise their children the way they want.

*fragment*

There is no other adult to share the experience.

*complete sentence*

Because there is no other adult to share the experience.

*fragment*

The following words can change a complete sentence (independent clause) into an incomplete sentence (a dependent clause).

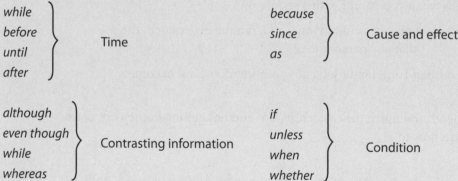

| while<br>before<br>until<br>after | } Time | because<br>since<br>as | } Cause and effect |
|---|---|---|---|
| although<br>even though<br>while<br>whereas | } Contrasting information | if<br>unless<br>when<br>whether | } Condition |

**NOTE:** If the dependent clause comes before the independent clause, a comma is necessary.

**EXAMPLES:** Even though they're a foster family, Yvonne and James feel like a "real" family.

Yvonne and James feel like a "real" family even though they're a foster family.

## 8 Completing Complex Sentences

**Using the subordinate conjunctions above, complete the following complex sentences. You may use some words more than once.**

1. _____ James has special needs, Yvonne keeps him on a regular schedule.

2. _____ you would like to participate in the research study, you will have to answer several questions about being a foster parent.

3. The researchers would not bother to ask that question _____ the answer was important to their study.

4. _____ he went to a powwow, James hadn't met many Native Americans. Now he has several Native American friends.

5. Babies tend to be adopted, _____ many older children end up in foster care.

6. _____ Sam has some trouble with his schoolwork, he is a very good reader.

7. Sam will have to go into foster care _____ someone adopts him soon.

8. _____ a person becomes a foster parent, he or she must go through a training program.

## 9 Using Complex Sentences

**Rewrite your answer to item 8, page 13, using compound and complex sentences.**

# Reading 3

## 1 Previewing

**Preview the reading on pages 18 to 19. Look at the title. Then read the first few paragraphs and the last paragraph. Study the picture.**

## 2 Thinking about the Topic

**In small groups, discuss your answers to the following questions.**

1. Who was primarily responsible for taking care of you when you were very young (e.g., your mother, your father, both parents, your grandparents, an aunt, etc.)?

2. What was your father's role in your family?

3. Do mothers and fathers parent differently? If so, how?

## 3 Making Predictions

**In small groups, discuss your answers to the following questions.**

1. What do you think the reading below will be about?

2. What details or examples might the author include to develop the main idea?

*Now read the text and answer the questions that follow.*

# Mr. Mom

Rocco burped. Then he spat. Rocco's dad, Billy Steel, was, until recently, an on-air personality for a San Francisco hard rock radio station. But despite decades of hanging around rock stars and heavy
5 metal musicians, Steel managed to avoid having anyone spit on him—until Rocco was born. Steel says he wears black all the time, and he's finding a lot of little white marks on his shoulders. Steel, 41, left his DJ job to stay home with Rocco while
10 his wife went back to work. He's happy with his decision. Steel said that it was difficult to leave a job he loved. But he thought about his own father—his role model—and decided that it was the right thing to do.

15 These days, Steel is not the only guy with shoulder stains. According to the U.S. Census Bureau, in 2005, there were approximately 143,000 stay-at-home dads in the United States, up from 98,000 in 2004. Those fathers cared for
20 an estimated 245,000 children younger than 15. Of these fathers, the biggest single chunk— 20 percent—were caring for preschool-aged children.

"It's not an easy transition for most parents,"
25 said Peter Baylies, author of *The Stay-at-Home Dad Handbook*. However, Baylies says that if they're persistent, it can actually work out better than women staying home, because moms have other ways to connect with their children. Baylies
30 explains that if a dad is working all the time, he doesn't have the bond that the mom had when she was pregnant for nine months. Baylies, who is himself a stay-at-home dad, adds that moms have a built-in bond. They come home from work
35 and get involved in a child's activities, while dads don't, according to Baylies.

The difficulties often lie in areas other than car-ing for the children. For example, men often don't consider all the household duties there are
40 once they agree to stay home. As many moms already know, it's like learning four or five jobs at once. Take Fred Safipour, for example. "You don't realize how much there is to do," he said. Safipour quit teaching tennis five years ago to
45 stay home with his son, John. His wife, Susan, is a magazine editor. Safipour grew up in Iran, one of five children raised by his mother while his dad traveled for work. He laughed when asked if any Iranian dads stayed home with the kids. He said it
50 was unheard of in those days.

According to Safipour, a lot of men say that they wish they could stay home, but they really don't understand just how much work it is. He feels that most dads think it's just a matter of going
55 outside and playing ball. Safipour believes these dads wouldn't last a week.

Then there's contending with the other moms. Safipour doesn't believe that society is ready for stay-at-home dads yet. He said that when he
60 would take his son to school, the moms would look at him strangely and avoid him. Also, he noted that at the playground, all the moms seemed to stick together and eye him from a distance.

That still shows a certain acceptance, compared
65 with the days when seeing a man with a child in the middle of the day prompted suspicion.

"I was the only man at a playground with my daughter, probably 26 or 27 years ago," said Dr. Michael Connor, a psychology professor at
70 California State University in Long Beach. "I was pushing her on the swing. Six mothers with their kids were there, and they called the police to say there was a man making inappropriate contact with a child."

75 Connor, who specializes in father-child relationships, said stay-at-home dads are obviously more common in comparatively wealthy suburban areas, where two incomes aren't always necessary. According to Connor, more dads
80 are willing to stay at home because fathers are finally figuring out what they're missing. He states that as women get higher salaries, it gives men the option. Furthermore, he adds, they often find that they like it.

85 However, Connor noted that not all moms adjust well. He was still in private practice when he met women having a harder time than their husbands with the change. He remembers one couple whose relationship ended when the man
90 began staying home.

"It happens routinely," he said. "Women would talk about how the child liked him better than her. But overall, having fathers involved is the best thing that can happen to a child. Being the
95 primary child-care provider isn't all that attractive to some men. But loving your children openly is one of the most masculine things you can do."

## 4 Comprehension Check

**Write your answers to the following questions.**

1. What do the 2005 U.S. Census Bureau figures indicate about stay-at-home fathers?

   _Approximately 143,000 stay-at-home dads in U.S. 45,000 more than 2004_

2. Why does Peter Baylies say that it's better for fathers to stay at home than for mothers to stay at home?

   _Because for dads stay at home required more work, because moms have different ways to connect with their children_

3. What aspect of the stay-at-home dad experience does Michael Connor's story illustrate?

   _Unusual, can be areason to ended reationships, dads can be more willing & they finally figuring_

4. In what type of family are you more likely to find a stay-at-home dad?

   _wealthy families. In my opinion that can depends at the cultural._

5. How does Connor feel about stay-at-home dads? How do you know?

   _Happy and in a correct way & "Being the primary child-care provider isn't all that attractive to some men. But loving your children openly is one of the most masculine things you can do._

6. List the pros and cons of being a stay-at-home dad, according to the article.

......................................................................................................................

......................................................................................................................

......................................................................................................................

......................................................................................................................

7. Write a one-paragraph summary of the pros and cons of being a stay-at-home dad.

......................................................................................................................

......................................................................................................................

......................................................................................................................

......................................................................................................................

......................................................................................................................

......................................................................................................................

## 5 Critical Analysis: Distinguishing Fact from Opinion

**Read the following statements and decide whether the information is a fact or an opinion. Check (✔) Fact or Opinion. Then write a brief explanation of your decision on the line. Discuss your answers with your classmates.**

1. According to the U.S. Census Bureau, in 2005, there were approximately 143,000 stay-at-home dads in the United States, up from 98,000 in 2004.

☐ a. Fact ☐ b. Opinion

......................................................................................................................

2. Those fathers cared for an estimated 245,000 children younger than 15.

☐ a. Fact ☐ b. Opinion

......................................................................................................................

3. Being a stay-at-home father is the right thing to do.

☐ a. Fact ☐ b. Opinion

......................................................................................................................

4. Society isn't ready for stay-at-home dads yet.

☐ a. Fact ☐ b. Opinion

......................................................................................................................

5. There were 80,000 stay-at-home dads in Japan in 2004.

☐ a. Fact ☐ b. Opinion

......................................................................................................................

## 6 Identifying Signal Words

Find the following sentences in "Mr. Mom." Discuss with a partner the purpose of each of the underlined signal words in relation to the ideas around them.

1. "It's not an easy transition for most parents," said Peter Baylies, author of *The Stay-at-Home Dad Handbook*. <u>However</u>, Baylies says that if they're persistent, it can actually work out better than women staying home, because moms have other ways to connect with their children. (para. 3)

2. The difficulties often lie in areas other than caring for the children. <u>For example</u>, men often don't consider all the household duties there are once they agree to stay home. (para. 4)

3. He said that when he would take his son to school, the moms would look at him strangely and avoid him. <u>Also</u>, he noted that at the playground, all the moms seemed to stick together and eye him from a distance. (para. 6)

4. He states that as women get higher salaries, it gives men the option. <u>Furthermore</u>, he adds, they often find that they like it. (para. 9)

5. <u>However</u>, Connor noted that not all moms adjust well. (para. 10)

## 7 Vocabulary in Context

Find and re-read the following sentences in "Mr. Mom." Then choose the best meaning for the underlined word or words.

1. But <u>despite</u> decades of hanging around rock stars and heavy metal musicians, Steel managed to avoid having anyone spit on him—until Rocco was born. (para. 1)
   a. even with
   b. because of
   c. in addition to

2. But he thought about his own father—his <u>role model</u>—and decided that it was the right thing to do. (para. 1)
   a. example of bad parenting
   b. example of how to behave
   c. example of how not to behave

3. Those fathers cared for <u>an estimated</u> 245,000 children younger than 15. (para. 2)
   a. at least
   b. about
   c. no more than

4. "It's not an easy <u>transition</u> for most parents," said Peter Baylies, author of *The Stay-at-Home Dad Handbook*. (para. 3)
   a. responsibility
   b. job
   c. change

5. However, Baylies says that if they're <u>persistent</u>, it can actually work out better than women staying home, because moms have other ways to connect with their children. (para. 3)

    **a.** consistent
    **b.** determined
    **c.** thoughtful

6. "Six mothers with their kids were there, and they called the police to say there was a man making <u>inappropriate</u> contact with a child." (para. 8)

    **a.** friendly
    **b.** illegal
    **c.** improper

7. He states that as women get higher salaries, it gives men the <u>option</u>. (para. 9)

    **a.** choice
    **b.** obligation
    **c.** support

8. "Being the <u>primary child-care provider</u> isn't all that attractive to some men." (para. 11)

    **a.** person most responsible for taking care of a child
    **b.** person least responsible for taking care of a child
    **c.** person not involved with taking care of a child

---

### Writing ⇢ *Sentence Types—Compound-Complex Sentences*

A **compound-complex sentence** consists of two or more independent clauses and one or more dependent clauses.

**EXAMPLES:**

- When Dr. Michael Connor was raising his daughter 26 years ago,
  dependent clause

  stay-at-home fathers were rare, but today they're more common.
  independent clause    independent clause

- Jack decided to be a stay-at-home dad, and this was a good arrangement for his
  independent clause    independent clause

  wife, although they sometimes disagreed about household chores.
      dependent clause

**NOTE:** Remember that commas connect two independent clauses and follow dependent clauses when they come before independent clauses.

## 8  Combining Sentences

**Using the conjunctions in parentheses, combine each set of sentences to form one compound-complex sentence. Put the clauses in any order that makes sense.**

1. Billy Steel spent many years working with rock stars.
   No one ever spat on him.
   Rocco Steel was born. (*but, until*)

2. Their son was born.
   Billy's wife went back to work.
   Billy left his job to stay at home with Rocco. (*after, but*)

3. Billy Steel had a great job.
   He decided to become a stay-at-home dad.
   He's happy with his decision. (*while, and*)

4. Men try hard to be good stay-at-home dads.
   It's often better than when women stay at home.
   Women have other ways of connecting with their children. (*if, because*)

5. Full-time parenting can be a difficult job.
   There are many household chores.
   Some women have a hard time with the transition. (*because, in addition*)

6. A dad takes his child to the park.
   The moms may ignore him.
   Some may even be suspicious. (*when, and*)

## 9  Using Compound-Complex Sentences

**Rewrite your answer to item 7, page 20, using compound-complex sentences.**

# Writing Focus

## Summarizing

A **summary** is a condensed restatement of the main ideas of a reading. Summaries are useful when you need to give an overview of a reading. They are also useful when preparing for examinations and recording key points from readings for a research paper.

- **What does a summary contain?**

A summary contains only the gist of the original and a few details. It does *not* contain all the information presented in the original. Most of the background information and explanations are omitted. Summaries are often about one-quarter the length of the original or less.

- **What steps do I follow to write a summary?**

1. Carefully read the original text; look up any difficult words that aren't clear from the context. It is essential to understand a reading before you summarize it.

2. Underline or highlight the sentences or phrases that contain the main idea or thesis of the reading. Rewrite the thesis in your own words. Then find the supporting details. The thesis and supporting details provide a rough outline of your summary.

3. Revise your outline, if necessary. Decide what to omit. Abridge and combine the information where possible. Present the ideas in the same order that they appeared in the reading. Leave out repetitions, examples, anecdotes, digressions, dialogue, quotations, parenthetical statements, figures of speech, jokes, minor descriptive details, and most statistics.

4. Write the summary in your own words, expressing the information in the outline. One way to ensure you are using your own words is to give an oral summary before you write. As you write, paraphrase sentences in the original by changing words to synonyms, varying the word order in your sentences, and combining sentences using compound, complex, and compound-complex sentence structures.

NOTE:    It is not always possible to give a synonym for a foreign or highly technical or specialized word or expression. In this case, it is acceptable to use the same words as in the original.

5. Connect the ideas in your summary using signal words.

6. Reread your summary and ensure that no essential information has been left out and that all the information comes from the reading. Also, make sure that all the words are your own.

## 1 Evaluating a Summary

**Read the following summary of "James" (page 11). Answer the questions with a partner.**

"James" is about the relationship between the author, Yvonne, who is a foster mother, and her child. The author finds that being a foster mother is just like being a "real" mother. She and her child are a "real" family. Yvonne looks after James's physical and emotional well-being, teaches him, provides for his material needs, and she loves him. Because James is Native American and Yvonne is not, she tries very hard to educate him about his culture; for example, by taking him to powwows. Yvonne is a single parent, which has both challenges and benefits. For example, she has no one to help her when she's tired, but on the other hand, she doesn't have to deal with a partner who might have different ideas about child-rearing. Because James has behavioral issues, Yvonne must provide him with limits, and she must also give special attention to maintaining a regular schedule for him. In sum, like all parents, Yvonne wonders how she is doing as a mother and realizes that parenting is a constant learning process.

**Questions**

1. How long is the summary? Is it about one-quarter the length of the original?

2. Does the summary express the main idea of the original? Underline it.

3. Does the summary express a few of the supporting details? Underline them.

4. Is there anything in the summary that should not be there, such as background information, quotations, anecdotes, or minor details?

5. Does the information in the summary appear in the same order that it appeared in the original?

6. Is the summary written in the author's own words? Find in the original an example of a word or expression that is expressed in a synonym in the summary. Find an example of a word in the original for which the summary author has *not* given a synonym. Find one example of a sentence in the original that is paraphrased in the summary.

7. Does the summary contain signal words? Find three and explain their purpose.

8. Are there any complex or compound-complex sentences in the summary? Find one and identify the independent and dependent clause(s).

## 2 Writing a Summary

**Write a summary of "Mr. Mom" following the guidelines above. The comprehension questions on page 19 will help you understand the main points of the reading; use them as an outline for your summary. As you write, remember to use signal words and vary your sentences (use compound, complex, and compound-complex sentences).**

## 3 After You Write

**Answer the following questions about your summary and then revise it.**

1. How long is the summary? Is it about one-quarter the length of the original?

2. Does the summary express the main idea of the original?

3. Does it express a few of the supporting details?

4. Is there anything in the summary that should not be there, such as background information, quotations, anecdotes, or minor details?

5. Does the information in the summary appear in the same order that it appeared in the original?

6. Is the summary written in your own words?

7. Does the summary contain signal words?

8. Are there any compound, complex, or compound-complex sentences in the summary?

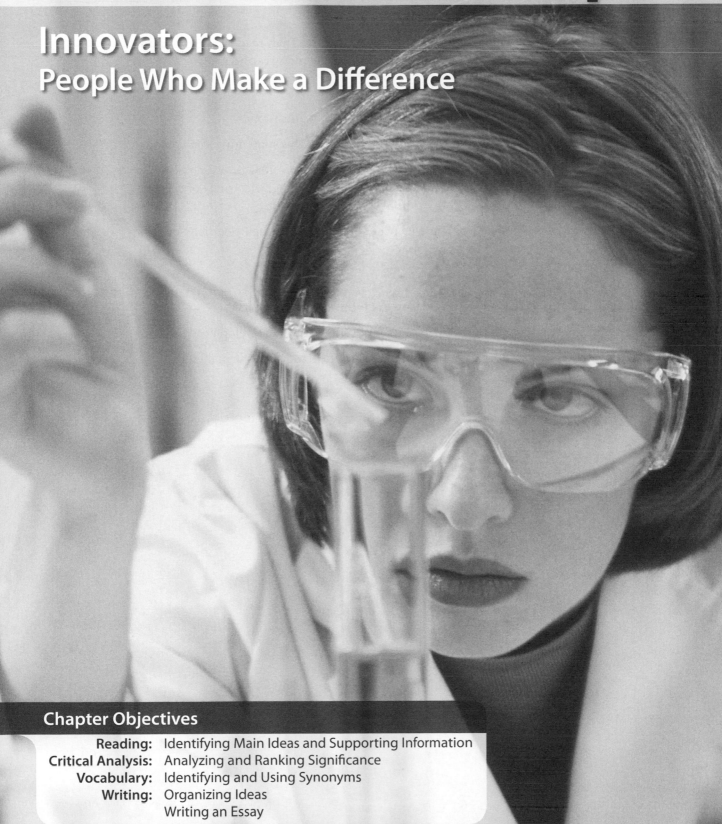

# Chapter 2

# Innovators:
## People Who Make a Difference

## Chapter Objectives

**Reading:** Identifying Main Ideas and Supporting Information
**Critical Analysis:** Analyzing and Ranking Significance
**Vocabulary:** Identifying and Using Synonyms
**Writing:** Organizing Ideas
Writing an Essay

# Reading 1

## 1  Previewing

Preview the reading on pages 29 to 30. Look at the title. Then read the introduction, the bold headings, and the last paragraph. Look at the pictures and captions.

## 2  Thinking about the Topic

In small groups, discuss your answers to the following questions.

1. Where does your water and electricity come from? Is this something that you often think about? Why or why not?

2. In what parts of the world might it be difficult to get enough electricity or clean water?

3. What might be some of the consequences of not having enough electricity or clean water?

## 3  Making Predictions

In small groups, discuss your answers to the following questions.

1. What do you think is the main idea of "Innovations for the Developing World"?

2. What details or examples might the author include to develop the main idea?

*Now read the text and answer the questions that follow.*

# Innovations for the Developing World

Engineer and inventor Dean Kamen is puzzling over a new equation these days. An estimated 1.1 billion people in the world don't have access to clean drinking water, and an estimated 1.6 billion don't have electricity. Those figures add up to a big problem for the world—and an equally big opportunity for entrepreneurs[1]. To solve the problem, he's invented two devices, each about the size of a washing machine. One is a generator that can provide much-needed power in rural villages. The other is a water-cleaning machine. In addition, Kamen is delivering these new technologies using an entrepreneurial economic model with proven success in the developing world.

## Lighting the Darkness

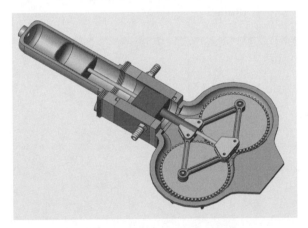

Prototype of Kamen's power generator

Kamen is testing the devices in real-world situations. For example, last year, prototypes[2] of Kamen's power machines went through a six-month field trial in two villages in Bangladesh. The power generator proved to be ideal for the developing world. According to Kamen, it runs on anything that burns. In Bangladesh, the electric generator is powered by an easily obtained local fuel: cow dung. Each machine continuously outputs a kilowatt of electricity. That may not sound like much, but it is enough to light 70 energy-efficient bulbs. As Kamen puts it, "If you judiciously use a kilowatt, each villager can have a nighttime."

This is a significant innovation for most of the developing world. How? To understand the significance, think of a satellite picture of the earth at night—it shows large areas of darkness across Southeast Asia, the Middle East, and Africa. For the people living there, a simple lightbulb would mean an extension of both their productivity and their leisure time.

## Cleaning Water

Kamen's other innovation is his water-cleaning machine, which he calls the Slingshot. The Slingshot works by taking in contaminated water—even raw sewage—and separating out the clean water by vaporizing it. The machine then shoots the remaining sludge back out through a plastic tube. Kamen thinks the Slingshot could be paired with the generator and run off the other machine's waste heat. Compared to building big power and water plants, Kamen's approach has the virtue of simplicity. He even created an instruction sheet to go with each Slingshot. It contains one step: just add water, any water. Step 2 might be to add an entrepreneur.

Kamen's water-cleaning machine

## Creating Entrepreneurs

The real invention here may be the economic model that Kamen hopes to use to distribute the

machines. Kamen has joined forces with Iqbal
55 Quadir, the founder of Grameen Phone, the
largest cell phone company in Bangladesh. The
distribution model for the power generator is
fashioned after the Grameen Phone business—
already in place in Bangladesh—in which village
60 entrepreneurs (mostly women) are given micro-
loans[3] to purchase a cell phone and service.
The women, in turn, charge other villagers to
make calls. Grameen Phone has 200,000 rural
entrepreneurs who are selling telephone services
65 in their communities.

Quadir and Kamen's vision is to replicate this
model with electricity. For example, during the
test in Bangladesh, Kamen's generators created
three entrepreneurs in each village: one to run
70 the machine and sell the electricity, one to collect
dung from local farmers and sell it to the first
entrepreneur, and a third to lease out lightbulbs

(and presumably, in the future, other appliances)
to the villagers.

75 Quadir believes that distributing the machines
in a decentralized fashion will be more beneficial
for the country than centralizing the technology.
Instead of putting up a 500-megawatt power plant
in a developing country, he argues, it would be
80 much better to place 500,000 one-kilowatt power
plants in villages all over the place, because then
you would create many more entrepreneurs.

---

**1 entrepreneurs:** people who start
new businesses

**2 prototypes:** models or
examples that work but aren't
the finished product

**3 micro-loans:** very small
loans—for example, of a few
dollars

## 4 Comprehension Check

**Write your answers to the following questions.**

1. What problem does Dean Kamen want to solve?

   _The problem is the estimated people with access problems to basic things like clean drinking water (1.1 billion people) and electricity (1.6 billion people)._

2. What two solutions does Kamen have?

   _• Lighting the darkness → power generator_
   _• Cleaning water → cleaning water machine_

3. How much power does Kamen's generator provide?

   _Each machine continuosly outputs a kilowatt of electricity, its enought to light 70 energy-efficient bulbs. (A kilowatt of electricy_

4. Why is the generator so well-suited to a country like Bangladesh?

   _Its easily obtained local fuel like cow dung_

5. What are the benefits of the generator? In other words, what does Kamen mean
   when he says, "If you judiciously use a kilowatt, each villager can have a nighttime"?

   _"A simple lightbulb would mean an extension of both their productivity and their leisure time."_

6. Explain in your own words how the Slingshot works.

..................................................................................................................................

..................................................................................................................................

7. Explain in your own words why the Slingshot is well-suited to the developing world.

..................................................................................................................................

8. What is Kamen's "real invention"? (para. 5)

..................................................................................................................................

## Critical Analysis → *Analyzing Significance*

**Analyzing significance** is a kind of critical analysis. Analyzing significance means judging importance. When you analyze the significance of something—for example, an invention—you determine how important it is. To do this, you think of both the actual and the possible effects of the invention. You look at the facts already on record regarding how the invention has helped people or improved the world in some way. You also think about its potential effects—how it might help the world in the future.

## 5 Critical Analysis: Analyzing Significance

**In small groups, discuss your answers to the following questions.**

1. According to the article, is there evidence that Kamen's inventions have already helped anyone? How do you know?

2. How might Kamen's inventions help people in the future?

3. On a scale of 1 (very important) to 5 (not important), how important are Kamen's inventions?

4. Think of four recent inventions or innovations, such as a new car design, a scientific discovery, a new type of drug, or a new entertainment technology. Add Kamen's inventions to your list and compare them with each of the other four items. Which item is more important? Rank the items in your list from 1 (most important) to 5 (least important).

## Vocabulary → *Identifying Synonyms*

**Synonyms** are words or phrases that have the same (or nearly the same) meaning.

EXAMPLE:   To solve the problem, he's invented two <u>devices</u>.

→ To solve the problem, he's invented two <u>machines</u>.

*Machines* is a synonym for *devices* in this sentence. However, synonyms do not always have the same meaning in all senses; they cannot always be used in the same context. For instance, the word *devices* (para. 1) can also mean methods or plans; in other words, not concrete objects.

Identifying synonyms helps you understand new words and expand your vocabulary. An especially useful tool is a thesaurus, which is a dictionary of synonyms. Thesauruses are written for the specific purpose of grouping words with similar meanings.

## 6  Identifying Synonyms

The following is a list of synonyms for words in the reading. Find the original word that matches the synonym in meaning and write it on the line.

1. necessary (para. 1): ......................................................................................

2. test (para. 2): .............................................................................................

3. yields (para. 2): ..........................................................................................

4. carefully (para. 2): ......................................................................................

5. polluted (para. 4): .......................................................................................

6. repeat (para. 6): ..........................................................................................

7. giving out (para. 7): .....................................................................................

8. manner (para. 7): ........................................................................................

### Reading ➡ *Identifying Main Ideas and Supporting Information*

The **main idea** is the central or controlling idea of a piece of writing or paragraph. Recognizing main ideas is an important reading skill. A sentence that expresses the main idea of a paragraph is called a **topic sentence**. Main ideas can be in various places in the paragraph: at the beginning, in the middle, or at the end. In addition, the main idea is sometimes simply implied.

A well-written paragraph contains not only a main idea but also **supporting information** such as a description, an explanation, and facts.

In order to understand or to identify main ideas as you read, ask yourself the following questions:

1. What is the main point that the writer is trying to make?

2. What does the writer want me to understand or to remember about this topic?

3. How does the writer develop or advance his or her main point?

For example, the main idea of paragraph 7 in "Innovations for the Developing World" is that Quadir thinks it will be better for Bangladesh not to centralize the new technology. This idea is expressed in the first sentence of that paragraph. The supporting information consists of an example that illustrates how 500,000 one-kilowatt power plants are better than one 500-megawatt power plant.

## 7 Identifying Main Ideas

Find the main idea of the following paragraphs in "Innovations for the Developing World." Underline the sentence that expresses the main idea (the topic sentence). On the line next to the paragraph number, state the main idea in your own words. You will use the "Supporting info" line in the next activity.

**1.** Para. 2: _____

Supporting info: _____

**2.** Para. 3: _____

Supporting info: _____

**3.** Para. 4: _____

Supporting info: _____

**4.** Para. 5: _____

Supporting info: _____

**5.** Para. 6: _____

Supporting info: _____

## 8 Identifying Supporting Information

Find supporting information for each of the main ideas in Activity 7. On the "Supporting info" lines above, state in your own words at least one example of supporting information and indicate the type of support it is—examples, details, facts, or explanations.

### Writing ➡ *Organizing Ideas*

It's a good idea to organize your ideas before you write. One way to do this is to use a **graphic organizer**. A graphic organizer gives you a way to see how ideas are related to each other, especially how main ideas are related to supporting information.

Here's an example of one type of graphic organizer:

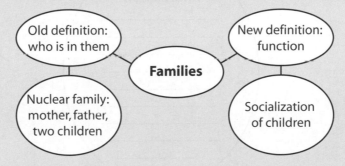

In this example, you can see that the topic is families, the two main ideas are the old and new definitions for the family, and each main idea has an example.

There are many types of graphic organizers. Choose the one that works best for your topic or your style of thinking.

## 9 Organizing Ideas

Complete the following graphic organizer with information from "Innovations for the Developing World."

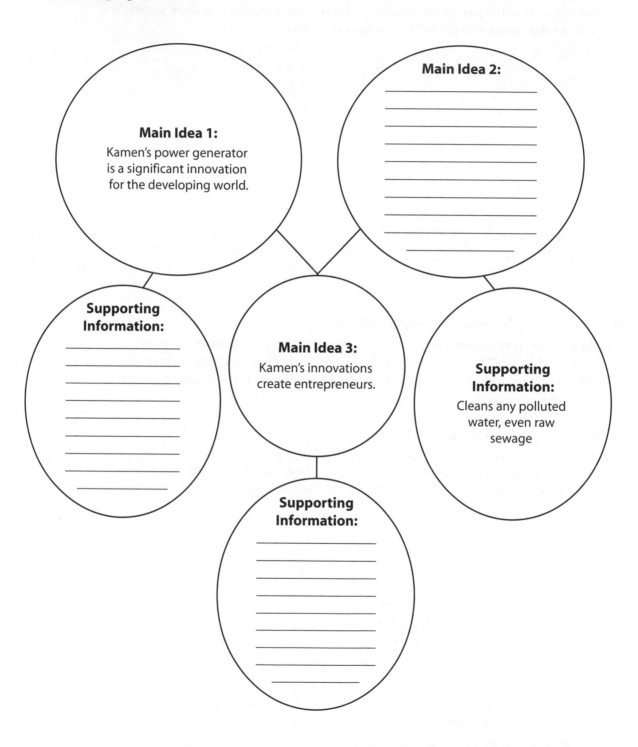

**Main Idea 1:**
Kamen's power generator is a significant innovation for the developing world.

**Main Idea 2:**

**Supporting Information:**

**Main Idea 3:**
Kamen's innovations create entrepreneurs.

**Supporting Information:**
Cleans any polluted water, even raw sewage

**Supporting Information:**

## 10 Writing a Summary

Use the graphic organizer to write a summary of "Innovations for the Developing World." Follow the guidelines for writing a summary on page 24 of Chapter 1.

# Reading 2

## 1 Previewing

Preview the reading on pages 36 to 38. Look at the title. Then read the introduction, the headings, and the last paragraph. Look at the pictures and captions.

## 2 Thinking about the Topic

In small groups, discuss your answers to the following questions.

1. What kind of paintings do you like? Give the names of some artists and/or titles of your favorite pictures. What time period(s) are they from?

2. Compare an older painting style to a modern one. For example, look at a painting from hundreds of years ago and a modern painting. How are they different in terms of subject matter and painting style?

3. Where do artists get ideas for their subjects? What might influence their painting style?

## 3 Making Predictions

In small groups, discuss your answers to the following questions.

1. What do you think is the main idea of "Finding a New Way to Paint"?

2. What details or examples might the author include to develop the main idea?

*Now read the text and answer the questions that follow.*

# Finding a New Way to Paint

In Paris in 1874, fifty-five artists, founders of a movement they called Impressionism, held the first independent group show. Most of them—including Cézanne, Pissarro, Renoir, Degas,
5  Monet, Manet, and Morisot—had been rejected by the Salon, the annual French state-sponsored exhibition that offered the only real opportunity for artists to display and sell their work. Never mind, they told each other. At the Salon, paintings
10  were stacked three or four high and crowded too closely together on the walls. At their independent exhibition, mounted in what was formerly a photographer's studio, the artists could hang their works at eye level with space between them.

15  Although some people appreciated the new paintings, many did not. The critics and the public agreed the Impressionists couldn't draw, and their colors were vulgar. Their compositions were strange. Their short, slapdash brushstrokes made
20  their paintings practically illegible. Why didn't these artists take the time to finish their canvases, viewers wondered?

## A Break from the Past

Indeed, Impressionism broke every rule of the French Academy of Fine Arts, the conservative
25  school that had dominated art training and taste since 1648. Impressionist scenes of modern urban and country life were very different from the Academic approach to art: to teach moral lessons through historic, mythological, and religious
30  themes. This tradition, drawn from ancient Greek and Roman art, featured idealized images. Symmetrical compositions, hard outlines, and meticulously smooth paint surfaces characterized academic paintings.

25  These "Independents," as they preferred to be called, brought together a wide variety of

*The Death of Socrates*, Jacques-Louis David (1787)

influences, beliefs, and styles when they first exhibited and met in Paris cafes to discuss art. The Academy's rejection of them in part united them
40  as a group. But what characterizes Impressionistic art as a whole?

## New Subjects

The most significant thread that linked the Impressionists together was an interest in the world around them. For subject matter, they
45  looked to contemporary people at work and play. Most Impressionists were born in the bourgeoisie class, and this was the world they painted. "Make us see and understand, with brush or with pencil, how great and poetic we are in our cravats and our
50  leather boots," the French poet Charles Baudelaire challenged his friend Édouard Manet. Baudelaire's essay "The Painter of Modern Life" inspired other Impressionists to portray real-life themes, too. Degas found his subjects in the backstage scenes
55  of the opera and the ballet. Monet immortalized Paris railroad stations. Nearly all the Impressionist artists painted people hurrying through busy streets and enjoying their leisure time on the boulevard, at racetracks and cafe-concerts, and in
60  stores, restaurants, and parks.

However, it was not just city life that intrigued the Impressionists. Country themes appealed to them, too. Railroads gave people a new mobility. They could hop on a train and be in the countryside in
65 an hour. Commuters escaped from the crowded city to the suburbs that were beginning to appear around Paris. The Seine River, parks, and gardens provided recreational opportunities for weekend picnickers, swimmers, and boat parties, which
70 the Impressionists duly recorded. According to some art historians, one key to Impressionism's popularity was that the artist often put the viewer in the position of someone on holiday enjoying a beautiful scene. "Monet never painted weekdays,"
75 one critic noted wryly.

*Le Moulin de la Galette at Montmarte*, Utrillo

### Capturing the Moment

Another characteristic of the Impressionists was the desire to capture the moment, especially outdoors. Most Impressionists worked directly and spontaneously from nature. It was the painter
80 Camille Corot who first advised artists to "submit to the first impression" of what they saw—a real landscape without the contrived classical ruins or biblical parables of French Academic painting.

Capturing the moment meant that Impres-
85 sionists often depicted people in mid-task. Degas caught audience members at the opera watching each other instead of the stage and ballet dancers stretching or adjusting their costumes before a performance. Renoir's guitar player strums her
90 instrument by herself. Pissarro's Parisian pedestrians hurriedly cross the city streets.

A wish to capture nature's fleeting moments led many Impressionists to paint the same scene at different times and in different weather. They had
95 to work fast to capture the moment or to finish an outdoor painting before the light changed. Artists had often made quick sketches in pencil or diluted oil paint on location, but now the sketch became the finished work. Impressionist painters adopted
100 a distinctive style of rapid, broken brushstrokes: lines for people on a busy street or specks to recreate flowers in a meadow.

### New Ways with Color

Impressionism was also characterized by its innovative use of color. Advances in the fields of
105 optics and color theory fascinated these painters. Working outdoors, Impressionists rendered the play of sunlight and the hues of nature with a palette of bolder, lighter colors than Academy painters used. In 1666, Sir Isaac Newton had
110 shown that white light could be split into many colors—including the three primary colors, red, blue, and yellow—by a prism. The Impressionists learned how to create the prismatic colors with a palette of pure, intense pigments and white. Unlike
115 Academy painters, who covered their canvases with a dark underpainting, Impressionists worked on unprimed white canvas or a pale gray or cream background for a lighter, brighter effect.

Michel-Eugene Chevreul's 1839 book *On the*
120 *Law of Simultaneous Contrast of Colors* guided the Impressionist practice of laying down strokes of pure, contrasting colors. Chevreul found that colors change in relation to the other colors near them. Complementary colors, or those directly opposite
125 each other on his color wheel, create the most intense effects when placed next to each other, he wrote. Red-green or blue-orange combinations cause an actual vibration in the viewer's eye so that color appears to leap off the canvas. No
130 wonder viewers react emotionally to the glittering sunlight on Monet's rivers or the splash of orange costume on Degas's ballet dancers. "I want my red

to sound like a bell!" Renoir said. "If I don't manage it at first, I put in more red, and also other colors, until I've got it."

### The Appeal of Impressionism

Many Impressionists had difficulty selling their art. Some reverted to Academic styles in order to earn a living; some lived in extreme poverty. Finally, in the 1880s and '90s, the world that the Impressionists painted began to accept them. Wealthy art collectors started buying their paintings. What caused the public finally to accept Impressionism? "Ironically," writes art historian Ann Dumas, "the Impressionists' former status as renegades enhanced their appeal to ... the bourgeois collector ... [It was] a new art for a new class that wanted images of the world they inhabited."

Impressionist painting remains popular today, most likely due to its broadly appealing color, spontaneity, and freshness.

## 4 Comprehension Check

**Write your answers to the following questions.**

1. How did the independent exhibition differ from the Salon exhibition?

   ...................................................................................................................

   ...................................................................................................................

2. What was the reason that the group of artists held the independent exhibition in the first place?

   ...................................................................................................................

   ...................................................................................................................

3. Describe the characteristics of Academic art.

   ...................................................................................................................

   ...................................................................................................................

   ...................................................................................................................

4. Explain in your own words the three main characteristics of Impressionist art and give two examples from the reading of each characteristic.

   1st characteristic: ..............................................................................

   Examples: ..............................................................................................

   ...................................................................................................................

   2nd characteristic: ............................................................................

   Examples: ..............................................................................................

   ...................................................................................................................

   3rd characteristic: ............................................................................

   Examples: ..............................................................................................

   ...................................................................................................................

5. Explain in your own words Baudelaire's challenge to Manet. What was he asking the Impressionists to do? (para. 5)

........................................................................................................................

........................................................................................................................

........................................................................................................................

6. Explain in your own words the painter Corot's advice to "submit to the first impression." How does this describe one aspect of Impressionist art? (para. 7)

........................................................................................................................

........................................................................................................................

7. Explain in your own words how Chevreul's book on color influenced Impressionist art. (para. 11)

........................................................................................................................

........................................................................................................................

........................................................................................................................

8. According to the reading, why might Impressionist art be popular today?

........................................................................................................................

........................................................................................................................

## 5 Critical Analysis: Analyzing Significance

**In small groups, discuss your answers to the following questions.**

1. In your opinion, does art help the world? How?

2. On a scale of 1 (very important) to 5 (not important), how important was the invention of Impressionism?

3. Compare Kamen's two inventions with the development of Impressionism. Which is more important? Why?

4. How does Impressionism compare with the items you listed on page 31? Add it to your list and re-rank the items from 1 (most important) to 5 (least important).

## Vocabulary ⇒ *Categorizing Synonyms*

**Categorizing synonyms** is putting them into groups of related meanings. Associating groups of synonyms with the same general meaning can help you understand and remember them better. Study the following examples of related words from "Innovations for the Developing World."

| Technology | Example | Experiment |
|---|---|---|
| device | model | trial |
| machine | prototype | test |

## 6 Categorizing Synonyms

Study the following words from "Finding a New Way to Paint." Then, in the chart below, put the words in categories. Word form (for example, verbs and nouns) doesn't matter, as long as the words have similar meanings. Some sample entries have been done for you.

| | |
|---|---|
| (to) capture, capturing, caught | (to) paint |
| coloring | (to) portray |
| depicted | recorded |
| to display, a display | rendered |
| exhibit, exhibition | scenes |
| hue | shade |
| images | show |
| immortalize, immortalized | subject |
| (to) mount, mounted | theme |
| pigment | tint |

| Show in a Picture | Show (Art) to the Public | Subject Matter | Color |
|---|---|---|---|
| to paint<br>immortalize, immortalized | to display, a display<br>to mount, mounted | theme<br>subject | hue<br>pigment |

## 7  Using Synonyms

**Replace the underlined words or groups of words with a synonym from the chart above. Use a different form of the word, if necessary.**

1. The first underline{showing} of Impressionist art occurred in Paris in 1874.

2. The Impressionists underline{showed} their work in a space that was formerly a photographer's studio.

3. Impressionists liked to underline{paint} scenes of everyday life, such as people hurrying through a busy street or enjoying leisure time at a park.

4. A good example of an Impressionist painting is *Le Moulin de la Galette*, in which Renoir underline{shows} a group of people at a dance.

5. underline{Showing} people in mid-task was a favorite Impressionist underline{subject}.

6. The underline{subject matter} of Impressionist works differed greatly from that of Academic paintings, which often underline{showed} historical or mythological underline{scenes}.

7. The use of pure, contrasting underline{colors} is one characteristic of Impressionist painting.

8. Degas added bright underline{colors} such as orange to his underline{depiction} of ballet dancers' costumes.

---

### Writing ➞ *Outlining*

**Outlining** is another way to organize your ideas before you write. It also helps you analyze the main ideas and supporting information in a reading. You can outline a paragraph or an entire reading.

To outline, state the main idea of each paragraph and then list the supporting information underneath it. You don't have to state the information in complete sentences; use notes. Use Roman numerals to number main ideas. Use capital letters for supporting ideas if you have more than one. Indent supporting information to show how the ideas and information in the reading are related to each other.

EXAMPLE:  Families **(Topic)**

    I.  Old definition: who is in them (**main idea** of 1st para.)

       Nuclear family: mother, father, two children (**supporting information** for 1st para.: example)

    II.  New definition: function (**main idea** of 2nd para.)
       A.  Socialization of children

       B.  Taking care of members (**supporting information** for 2nd para.: examples)

## 8  Analyzing an Outline

Read this partial outline of "Innovations for the Developing World" and answer the questions that follow.

### Innovations for the Developing World

II. Kamen's power generator is appropriate for developing world.

    A.  Runs on anything that burns; example: even cow dung

    B.  Continuously outputs 1 kilowatt of electricity

III. Generator is an important innovation.

    Much of developing world is dark at night.

IV. Kamen's water cleaner is appropriate for developing world.

    A.  Cleans any polluted water; example: cleans raw sewage

    B.  Simple to use

V. Kamen's inventions are distributed using an economic model appropriate for developing world.

    Distribution model for the power generator is fashioned after Grameen Phone business.

### Questions

1. What is the main idea of paragraph 2?

    .................................................................................................................................

    What kind of supporting information is there for this main idea?

    .................................................................................................................................

2. What is the main idea of paragraph 3?

    .................................................................................................................................

    What kind of supporting information is there for this main idea?

    .................................................................................................................................

3. What is the main idea of paragraph 4?

    .................................................................................................................................

    What kind of supporting information is there for this main idea?

    .................................................................................................................................

4. What is the main idea of paragraph 5?

    .................................................................................................................................

    What kind of supporting information is there for this main idea?

    .................................................................................................................................

## 9  Creating an Outline

**Complete the following outline of several paragraphs from "Finding a New Way to Paint."**

### Finding a New Way to Paint

II. Many did not appreciate the new paintings.

    A. ................................................................................................

    B. ................................................................................................

    C. ................................................................................................

    D. ................................................................................................

III. ................................................................................................

    A. Impressionist: modern urban and country life

    B. Academic: ...........................................................................

    V. One characteristic of Impressionists: interest in the world around them

    .................................................................................................

    .................................................................................................

    .................................................................................................

VIII. ................................................................................................

    A. Degas: audience members watching each other; dancers stretching, adjusting costumes

    B. Renoir's guitar player

    C. Pissarro's pedestrians crossing streets

    X. Impressionists' use of color

    A. ................................................................................................

    B. ................................................................................................

# Reading 3

## 1 Previewing

Preview the reading on pages 45 to 46. Look at the title. Then read the first paragraph and the last paragraph. Study the picture and caption.

## 2 Thinking about the Topic

In small groups, discuss your answers to the following questions.

1. Do you prefer modern architecture or traditional architecture? Why?

2. Think of one example of modern architecture in your community (or anywhere in the world) and describe it.

3. What does the building you described say about the person who designed it?

4. In general, what kind of person designs buildings? What characteristics do you think they have? What motivates them?

## 3 Making Predictions

In small groups, discuss your answers to the following questions.

1. Who do you think Frank Gehry is?

2. What do you think this reading will be about?

3. What details or examples might the author include to develop the main idea?

*Now read the text and answer the questions that follow.*

# Frank Gehry

According to Frank Gehry, it all started when he was a little boy growing up on Beverley Street in Toronto, Canada. His grandmother would go to a nearby woodshop to get wood for her
5  stove. The pieces she brought home had been cut into a variety of strange shapes. Before his grandmother burned the pieces of wood in her fire, she would sit on the floor with him and build cities. Today, Gehry is considered by many
10  to be one of the greatest architects of our time. His signature—artistic structures composed of seemingly unrelated and inconsistent forms made of nontraditional materials—is a reflection of his approach to architecture and his underlying
15  philosophy.

Collections of unusual forms, such as Gehry's Guggenheim Museum in Bilbao, Spain, are typical of much of his work. Gehry's style reflects both the process in which he engages as an
20  architect and his philosophy of the modern city and democracy. Gehry's way of working is to begin by listening closely to his clients. He takes note not only of their explicit requests but also of their body language and facial expressions
25  to give him cues as to their desires and wishes. Gehry then works as a sculptor, using his intuition to guide him in the creation of shapes and forms that will appeal to his client. According to art critic Calvin Tomkins, when he has created a
30  model that is similar to what his clients want, Gehry's own design process really begins. He experiments with the model, modifying forms and the relationships among the forms, pushing the model further and further. When describing
35  this process, Gehry has said, "The creative spirit flows from my childlike sense of the world, my sense of play and wonder."

The unusual forms in Gehry's work also embody his philosophy of the modern city and democracy.
40  According to Gehry, the unity and uniformity

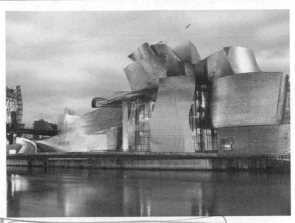

Guggenheim Museum, Bilbao, Spain

of the nineteenth-century city no longer exist; because our modern society is democratic, our cities are more chaotic. They reflect the pluralism within our society, and the forms within them
45  are "collisive"—clashing into each other. This new reality is expressed in the unusual and "collisive" shapes of Gehry's buildings, such as the Bilbao Guggenheim in Spain. Buildings like the Guggenheim are an expression of his view of
50  contemporary life.

In addition to their striking shapes, Gehry's structures are characterized by the use of unusual materials. Gehry often uses titanium, a material more frequently found in aircraft landing gear. He
55  chose titanium for the Guggenheim, for example, because "it has a wonderful characteristic of changing in the light. When it rains, it goes golden, so just when the grey skies come, which is a lot of the times in Bilbao, the building radiates."

60  Gehry has woven other unusual materials such as chain link into his designs. Again, the use of these materials reveals his thinking about life and architecture. According to Gehry himself, he wants to understand the materials that are
65  commonly used in our culture. "My goal as an architect is to take the 'culturally common'

materials I see being used in huge quantities and transform them into something better. I want to understand the materials and to use them, since 70 their use is inevitable anyway."

While Gehry's designs may at first seem strange and even jarring, they express his understanding of modern life. These designs are now inspiring a younger generation of architects, who, he hopes, 75 will be encouraged to take risks and express their own understanding through their work. In the meantime, we are left to enjoy and find our own meaning in Gehry's work, the art that is architecture.

## 4 Comprehension Check

**Write your answers to the following questions.**

1. What is the main idea of this article?
   a. Frank Gehry is the greatest architect of our time.
   b. Frank Gehry learned his skills from his grandmother when he was a small boy.
   c. Gehry's work reflects his approach to and philosophy about architecture.

2. How does the author of the article describe Gehry's architectural style?
   _Artistic structures are composed of unrelated forms that are made from non traditional materials_

3. Describe in your own words Gehry's process.
   _He had a natural talent, and He can find how important is can be read the body language or know exactly what is He people want and expected I using unusual materials._

4. Explain how Gehry's philosophy about the modern city is reflected in his designs.
   _Now the cities have less uniformity, and more space for free expression. He thinks city life style is chaotic, one infuses chaos in his designs_

5. In terms of Gehry's designs, what does "collisive" shapes mean? (para. 3)
   _The shapes in his designes collide into each other_

6. What else characterizes Gehry's architectural style?
   _Use the unusual materials. (Titanium)_

7. Describe in your own words Gehry's philosophy about the materials he uses.
   _"The use this materials reveals his thinking about life and architecture" the unusual materials can give to him buildings the different expressions, and can better different express him caos_ opinion

8. What influence does Gehry hope to have on young architects?
   _He hopes will be encouraged to take risks and express their own understanding through their work._

## 5 Critical Analysis: Analyzing Significance

**In small groups, discuss your answers to the following questions.**

1. How important is appearance in architecture? Does the way that buildings look matter? Why or why not?

2. Should architects have the freedom to design public buildings (such as museums) any way they want? Why or why not?

3. What effect does building design have on various aspects of life? For example, how do the size, shape, color, and other aspects of a structure such as an office building affect the people who work there?

4. Compare Gehry's work to Kamen's two inventions and the development of Impressionism. Which of the three is the most important? Why?

## 6 Vocabulary in Context

Find the following sentences in "Frank Gehry." Study the underlined words in context and provide a synonym for each.

1. His signature—artistic structures composed of seemingly unrelated and inconsistent forms made of nontraditional materials—is a reflection of his _approach to_ architecture and his underlying philosophy. (para. 1)

   *contribution*

   to come near or nearer to

2. His signature—artistic structures composed of seemingly unrelated and _inconsistent_ forms made of nontraditional materials—is a reflection of his approach to architecture and his underlying philosophy. (para. 1)

   *#'s*

   contrary, uncertain, incompatible, unpredictable

3. He takes note not only of their _explicit_ requests but also of their body language and facial expressions to give him cues as to their desires and wishes. (para. 2)

   *more especific*

   certain, clear, exact, definitive.

4. He experiments with the model, _modifying_ forms and the relationships among the forms, pushing the model further and further. (para. 2)

   *made changes.*

   alter, adjust, correct, revise

5. According to Gehry, the unity and _uniformity_ of the nineteenth-century city no longer exist; because our modern society is democratic, our cities are more chaotic. (para. 3)

   *Same - no difference.*

   conformity, equality, harmony.

6. Buildings like the Guggenheim are an expression of his view of _contemporary_ life. (para. 3)

   *actual*

   new, present day, recent.

7. "My goal as an architect is to take the 'culturally common' materials I see being used in huge quantities and transform them into something better. I want to understand the materials and to use them, since their use is _inevitable_ anyway." (para. 4)

   *you can't stop.*

   imminent, impeding, inexorable, necessary.

8. "My goal as an architect is to take the 'culturally common' materials I see being used in huge quantities and _transform_ them into something better." (para. 4)

   *change*

   alter, convert, mold, reconstruct.

# Writing Focus

## Writing an Essay

An **essay** is a series of paragraphs about a particular topic or subject. It has an introduction, several developmental paragraphs—called *body paragraphs*—and a conclusion.

An essay usually begins with an **introduction** that prepares the reader for the rest of the material by presenting information in a general-to-specific pattern.

- It begins with background information, which is general.
- It may include a *hook*, a device that stimulates the reader's interest. The hook might be a question, an anecdote, or a quotation.
- It then presents the thesis statement, which is specific. The thesis statement states the main idea of the entire essay and indicates the author's purpose in writing as well as his or her point of view.

The paragraphs that follow the introduction are called the **body** of the essay. Here, the writer develops the argument or point of view presented in the thesis statement. This development is in the form of supporting details such as examples, facts, reasons, descriptions, explanations, or opinions.

The **conclusion** usually restates the topic (specific), summarizes the main points, and adds a question or two for further reflection on the topic (general).

The diagram below shows how an essay is usually organized.

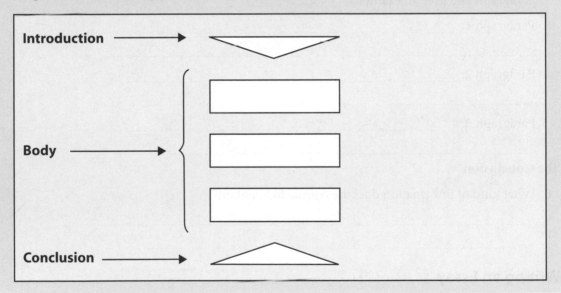

# 1  Analyzing an Essay

**Reread "Frank Gehry" and answer the following questions.**

## The Introduction

1. Is there a hook in the introduction? What kind of hook is it?

   _Personal story_

2. Find and underline the thesis statement. Restate it in your own words.

   _Frank Gehry created a new style, eagerly to reflect him_

## The Body _personal ideas_

3. How many body paragraphs are there?

   _3_

4. Underline the topic sentence of each body paragraph. Briefly state in your own words the main idea of each body paragraph.

   _#1 sure_

   _2. Him ideas change different relashonships inside the traditonall Architecture_

5. Indicate the kind of supporting information the writer provides in each body paragraph and give an example.

   Paragraph 1: _He experiments with the model, modifying forms abt the relinonships among the forms ... (BT)_

   Paragraph 2: _They reflect the pluralim withing our society, and the forms withing them are "collisive" clashing into each other_

   Paragraph 3: _He singunure artistic structures compose of seemindly ..._

## The Conclusion

6. What kind of information does the conclusion contain?

   _him expectations about the new generation) architecture work_

# 2  Writing an Essay

**You have read about and discussed innovators and innovations. Now write an essay of at least five paragraphs on one of the following topics. Outline your ideas before you write and remember to use synonyms and to vary your sentence types.**

- An innovative person who helped change someone's life

- An innovation that changed the world

- An innovation you would work on if money were no object

- A topic of your choice related to innovation

# 3   Preparing to Write

The following suggestions may help you plan and organize your paper.

1. Brainstorm for information. List all your ideas about the topic.

2. Choose the most relevant ideas; delete any ideas that do not connect to your topic.

3. Write down the main idea or thesis statement.

4. Use a graphic organizer or an outline to plan your essay. Include in it your thesis statement; your topic sentences or the main ideas of each body paragraph; and the examples, explanations, facts, or personal experiences that you will use to develop your ideas in each body paragraph. Think about how you might conclude your essay. Write notes, not complete sentences. Use the outline format below or create your own.

5. Write your first draft.

## Outline

Topic: .................................................................................................................

**Introduction**

    Thesis statement: ....................................................................................

.................................................................................................................

**Body**

    Paragraph 1 main idea and possible supporting information:

.................................................................................................................

.................................................................................................................

    Paragraph 2 main idea and possible supporting information:

.................................................................................................................

.................................................................................................................

    Paragraph 3 main idea and possible supporting information:

.................................................................................................................

.................................................................................................................

**Conclusion**

.................................................................................................................

## 4  After You Write

**Answer the following questions about your essay and then revise it.**

1. Does your introduction proceed from general to specific information?

2. Do you have a hook? What kind?

3. Does your thesis statement express the main idea of your essay?

4. Does the main idea of each body paragraph relate to your thesis statement?

5. Are the main ideas of each body paragraph thoroughly developed?

6. Does the conclusion make a logical and clear summary statement?

7. Did you use synonyms?

8. Is there a variety of sentence types?

## Chapter 3

# Natural Disasters

## Chapter Objectives

| | |
|---|---|
| **Reading:** | Scanning for Information |
| | Chronological Order |
| **Critical Analysis:** | Analyzing Causes and Effects |
| **Vocabulary:** | Identifying Suffixes and Prefixes |
| **Writing:** | Thesis Statements |
| | Describing a Process |

# Reading 1

## 1 Previewing

Preview the reading on pages 55 to 57. Look at the title. Then read the first few paragraphs, the headings, and the last paragraph.

### Reading ⇒ *Scanning for Information*

**Scanning** is looking for information quickly before or after you read a text. It's one way of previewing. You can scan for numbers, symbols, bold text, names, key words, or brief answers to questions.

**To scan**

**1.** Decide on what you want to find: a date; the name of a person or an organization; a place name; or a specific fact about a person, a place, or an event.

**2.** Predict what you will be looking for: capital letters, numbers, or symbols, for example.

**3.** Move your eyes quickly across the page—with the help of your finger or a pencil, if you want—looking only for the item you want to find.

**4.** Quickly check the context of the item for key words that match what you want to find.

EXAMPLE:

Read the following question:

How much has the average temperature increased over the last century?

To find the answer, look at the first paragraph of the passage. You know that you want to find a temperature increase, so you will be looking for a number. Scan the paragraph, looking for numbers. There are several, so quickly read the contexts to find the key words "over the last century."

The answer is about 1 degree Fahrenheit (0.6 degree Celsius).

## 2 Scanning for Information

Scan the "Climate Change" section of "Global Warming" to find answers to the following questions.

1. Will this article give you information on the trends in temperature change? Find an example.

   ...........................................................................................................................

2. What part of the world does this article focus on?

   ...........................................................................................................................

3. What is the source for this article's information?

   ...........................................................................................................................

4. What is one of the sources for statistics used in this article?

   ...........................................................................................................................

5. What time period does the article cover?

   ...........................................................................................................................

## 3 Thinking about the Topic

**In small groups, discuss your answers to the following questions.**

1. Do you have the impression that weather patterns are different today than they were in the past? If so, how are they different?

2. What do you already know about global warming?

3. What might be some of the effects of global warming? What might be some of the causes?

## 4 Making Predictions

**In small groups, discuss your answers to the following questions.**

1. What do you think is the main idea of "Global Warming"?

2. What details or examples might the author include to develop the main idea?

*Now read the text and answer the questions that follow.*

# Global Warming

Global warming is a hot topic that shows little sign of cooling down. Earth's climate *is* changing, but just how it's happening and our own role in the process are somewhat uncertain.

### Climate Change

5 There is little doubt that the planet is warming. Over the last century, the average temperature has climbed about 1 degree Fahrenheit (0.6 degree Celsius) around the world. The spring ice thaw in the Northern Hemisphere occurs 9
10 days earlier than it did 150 years ago, and the fall freeze now typically starts 10 days later. And the 1990s was the warmest decade since the mid-1800s, when record keeping started. At the time of this writing, the hottest years recorded
15 were 1998, 2002, 2003, 2001, and 1997. The multinational Arctic Climate Impact Assessment (ACIA) report recently concluded that in Alaska, western Canada, and eastern Russia, average temperatures have increased as much as 4 to 7
20 degrees Fahrenheit (3 to 4 degrees Celsius) in the past 50 years. The rise is nearly twice the global average. In Barrow, Alaska (the northernmost city in the United States), average temperatures rose more than 4 degrees Fahrenheit (2.5 to 3

25 degrees Celsius) in 30 years. The United Nations' Intergovernmental Panel on Climate Change (IPCC) projects that global temperatures will inevitably rise an additional 3 to 10 degrees Fahrenheit (1.6 to 5.5 degrees Celsius) by the end
30 of the century.

Over the last million years, Earth has fluctuated between colder and warmer periods. The shifts have occurred in roughly 100,000-year intervals thought to be regulated by sunlight.
35 Earth's sunlight quota depends upon its orbit and celestial orientation. But changes have also occurred more rapidly in the past—and scientists hope that these changes can tell us more about the current state of climate change. During the
40 last ice age, approximately 70,000 to 11,500 years ago, ice covered much of North America and Europe—yet sudden, sometimes drastic, climate changes occurred during the period. Greenland ice cores indicate one spike in which the area's
45 surface temperature increased by 15 degrees Fahrenheit (9 degrees Celsius) in just 10 years.

Where do scientists find clues to past climate change? The tale is told in remnant materials like glacial ice and moraines, pollen-rich mud, stalagmites, the rings of corals and trees, and ocean sediments that yield the shells of microscopic organisms. Human history yields clues as well, through records like ancient writings and inscriptions, gardening and vintner records, and the logs of historic ships.

## Melting Ice

Rising temperatures have a dramatic impact on Arctic ice, which serves as a kind of air conditioner at the top of the world. Since 1978, Arctic sea ice area has shrunk by some 9 percent per decade and has thinned as well. ACIA projects that at least half of the Arctic's summer sea ice will melt by the end of the century and that the Arctic region is likely to warm 7 to 13 degrees Fahrenheit (4 to 7 degrees Celsius) during the same time. Vast quantities of fresh water are tied up in the world's many melting glaciers. When Montana's Glacier National Park was created in 1910, it held some 150 glaciers. Now fewer than 30 greatly shrunken glaciers remain. Tropical glaciers are in even more trouble. The legendary snows at the peak of Tanzania's Mount Kilimanjaro, 19,340 feet (5,895 meters) high, have melted by some 80 percent since 1912 and could be gone by 2020.

In the Arctic, the impacts of a warming climate are being felt already. Coastal indigenous communities report shorter periods of sea ice, which fail to temper ocean storms and their destructive coastal erosion. Increased snow and ice melt has caused rivers to be higher, while thawing permafrost has wreaked havoc on roads and other infrastructure. Some communities have had to move from historic coastline locations. Sea ice loss is devastating for various species, such as polar bears and ringed seals in the Arctic and penguins in the Antarctic.

## Sea Levels

Melting ice can also mean higher sea levels. Sea levels have risen and fallen many times over the Earth's long geological history. According to the IPCC, the average global sea level has risen by 4 to 8 inches (10 to 20 cm) over the past century. The IPCC's 2001 report projects that sea level could rise between 4 and 35 inches (10 to 89 cm) by the end of the century. Such rises could have major effects for coastal dwellers. A 1.5-foot (50-centimeter) sea level rise in flat coastal areas would cause a typical coastline retreat of 150 feet (50 meters). Worldwide, some 100 million people live within 3 feet (1 meter) of mean sea level. Rises of just 4 inches (10 centimeters) could promote flooding in many South Sea islands, while in the United States, Florida and Louisiana are at risk. The Indian Ocean nation of Maldives has a maximum elevation of only 8 feet (2.5 meters). Construction of a sea wall around the capital, Male, was driven by vulnerability to the rising tides.

## Greenhouse Gases

Since the 1860s, increased industrialization and shrinking forests have helped raise the atmosphere's $CO_2$ level by almost 100 parts per million—and Northern Hemisphere temperatures have followed suit. Increases in temperatures and greenhouse gases have been even sharper since the 1950s.

Water vapor is the most important greenhouse gas. Carbon dioxide, methane, and nitrous oxide also contain heat and help keep Earth's temperate climate balanced in the cold void of space. Human activities, burning fossil fuels and clearing forests, have greatly increased concentrations by producing these gases faster than plants and oceans can soak them up. The gases linger in the atmosphere for years, meaning that even a complete halt in emissions would not immediately stop the warming trend they promote.

## Plants and Animals

Studies show that many European plants now flower a week earlier than they did in the 1950s and lose their leaves five days later. Biologists report that many birds and frogs are breeding earlier in the season. An analysis of 35 nonmigratory butterfly species showed that two-thirds now range 2 to 150 miles (3.5 to 240 kilometers) farther north than they did a few decades ago.

By 2050, rising temperatures, exacerbated by human-produced carbon dioxide and other greenhouse gases, could send more than a million of Earth's land-dwelling plants and animals down the road to extinction. Coral reefs worldwide are "bleaching," losing key algae and resident organisms, as water temperatures rise above 85 degrees Fahrenheit (29.5 degrees Celsius) through periods of calm, sunny weather. Scientists worry that rapid climate change could inhibit the ability of many species to adapt within complex and interdependent ecosystems.

135
140
145

### Is It All Bad News?

The effects of a warming globe may not be entirely negative. Heating costs could decrease for those in colder climates, while vast marginal agricultural areas in northern latitudes might become more viable. Arctic shipping and resource extraction operations could also benefit— summer sea ice breakup in Hudson Bay already occurs two to three weeks earlier than it did half a century ago. But many species could be hit hard—including humans. The most vulnerable are peoples living in the far North, those perched along the world's coasts, and millions dependent on subsistence agriculture subject to the vagaries of a changing climate.

150
155

## 5  Comprehension Check

**Write your answers to the following questions.**

1. Is climate change a new occurrence? Find the information in the passage that supports your answer.

   *No, Over the last century, the average temperature has climbed about 1 degree F (0.60°) around the world.*

2. How are temperatures changing today? Find at least two examples in the passage that support your answer.

   *✱ Melting Ice.*
   *✱ Sea levels.*

3. Where do scientists find clues to past climate change?

   *In materials like glacial ice and moraines, pollen-rich mud, stalagmites, the rings of corals and trees, and ocean sediments that...*

4. What are greenhouse gases? Where do they come from?

   *gases to captain heat and help keep Earth's temperate climate balanced in the cold void of space. Human activities...*

5. What does the author mean by "The effects of a warming globe may not be entirely negative"? Do you agree? Why or why not?

   *Our planet can answered ef a warming globe effects, but the changes can have huge consecuentes.*

## 6　Critical Analysis: Analyzing Causes and Effects

**In small groups, discuss your answers to the following questions.**

1. What effects is global warming having on Arctic ice?

2. What effects does melting ice have?

3. What effect is global warming having on plants and animals right now? What effects might there be in the future?

4. What might be one of the causes of increasing temperatures? Give specific answers.

5. In your opinion, can global warming be stopped? If yes, how?

## 7 Identifying Suffixes

In "Global Warming," find examples of words that contain the suffixes in the chart below. Then, from the examples, identify the part of speech created by adding each suffix. The first one has been done for you.

| Suffixes | | | |
|---|---|---|---|
| Suffix | Meaning | Examples | Part of Speech |
| al | relating to | global, celestial | adjective |
| ance, ence | instance of an action | | |
| er, or | person or thing connected with | | |
| ic | having the form of | | |
| ity, ty | quality or state | | |
| ly | in the manner of | | |
| ment | means or result of an action; also: action, process | | |
| ous, ious | having the qualities of | | |
| tion, ation | action or process | | |
| ist | person whose job or belief is | | |
| able, ible | having the ability | | |

## 8 Identifying Prefixes

In "Global Warming," find examples of words that include the following prefixes. Then use your knowledge of prefixes and the examples to fill in the meaning of the prefixes.

| Prefixes | | |
|---|---|---|
| Prefix | Meaning | Examples |
| de | | |
| in | | |
| inter | | |
| non | | |
| un | | |

## 9 Identifying Main Ideas

Reread "Global Warming." As you read, note in the margin the main idea of each paragraph. Compare your notes with a partner.

## 10 Writing a Summary

Write a summary of "Global Warming." Use the main ideas you noted in Activity 9 above. Follow the guidelines for writing a summary on page 24 of Chapter 1.

# Reading 2

## 1 Previewing

Preview the reading on pages 61 to 63. Look at the title. Then read the first paragraph, the last paragraph, and the headings.

## 2 Scanning for Information

Scan the first paragraph of "Disaster Reduction" to find answers to the following questions.

1. How many people died as a result of natural disasters in the 1990s?

   ....................................................................................................................................

2. How many people died as a result of natural disasters in the 1970s?

   ....................................................................................................................................

3. How many people have been affected by natural disasters in the past decade?

   ....................................................................................................................................

4. What percent of the world's population lives in an area that was affected by a natural disaster between 1980 and 2000?

   ....................................................................................................................................

5. What organization determined the percentage referred to in item 4 above?

   ....................................................................................................................................

6. Where did the December 2004 tsunami occur?

   ....................................................................................................................................

## 3 Thinking about the Topic

In small groups, discuss your answers to the following questions.

1. What are natural disasters? Make a list of as many kinds as you can think of.

2. Do you have the impression that there are more natural disasters today than there were in the past? Why or why not?

3. When there's a natural disaster, who often suffers the most?

## 4 Making Predictions

In small groups, discuss your answers to the following questions.

1. What do you think is the main idea of "Disaster Reduction"?

2. What details or examples might the author include to develop the main idea?

*Now read the text and answer the questions that follow.*

# Disaster Reduction

## Natural Disasters: A Heavy Price to Pay

Natural disasters are happening more often and are having an ever more dramatic impact on the world in terms of both their human and their economic costs. While the number of lives lost has declined in the past 20 years—800,000 people died as a result of natural disasters in the 1990s, compared with 2 million in the 1970s—the number of people affected has risen. Over the past decade, the total number of people affected by natural disasters has tripled to 2 billion. According to the United Nations (UN) Bureau for Crisis Prevention and Recovery, some 75 percent of the world's population lives in an area affected at least once by an earthquake, a tropical cyclone, flooding, or drought between 1980 and 2000. An estimated 250,000 to 300,000 people were killed in the December 2004 tsunami in the Indian Ocean or were still missing six months later. In addition, millions of lives were upturned, socially and economically, by the tsunami's impact.

The International Federation of the Red Cross and Red Crescent Societies, which publishes a World Disasters Report annually, calculates that from 1994 to 1998, reported disasters averaged 428 per year. From 1999 to 2003, this figure shot up by two-thirds to an average of 707 natural disasters each year. The biggest rise occurred in developing countries, which suffered an increase of 142 percent. According to a 2004 report by Munich Reinsurance Company, an international insurance company, in 2003 there were approximately 700 natural disasters, which killed an estimated 75,000 people and caused about U.S. $65 billion worth of damage.

## Increased Frequency: A Changing Environment

Since 1988, the Centre for Research on the Epidemiology of Disasters has kept a worldwide emergency database of disasters called EM-DAT. The database contains essential information on more than 14,000 disasters in the world, dating from 1900 to the present.

Natural disasters are divided into three specific groups: hydro-meterological, weather-related disasters such as floods and droughts; geophysical, such as earthquakes and tsunamis; and biological, such as epidemics and insect infestations.

EM-DAT's data show that over the past decade, the number of natural and technological disasters has risen sharply. Both hydro-meteorological and geophysical disasters have become more common, becoming 68 percent and 62 percent more frequent, respectively, over the last ten years. This reflects longer-term trends.

Weather-related disasters still outnumber geophysical disasters—by 9 to 1 over the past decade, according to the International Federation's analysis—while floods are the most-reported natural disasters in Africa, Asia, and Europe. Storms with high winds are most frequent in the Americas and Oceania.

The factors most often blamed for the increase in natural disasters are environmental degradation, climate change, population growth (in particular, unplanned urban growth), and the negative results of economic globalization.

## Poor Hardest-Hit When Disaster Strikes

Disasters are closely linked to poverty; they can wipe out decades of development in a matter of hours, in a manner that rarely happens in richer countries. The UN's Rapid Environmental Assessment of the impact of the December 2004 tsunami noted: "Disproportionately, many of the victims of this disaster were poor people who depended on eco-system services and natural resources for their livelihoods."

Poor people in developing countries are particularly vulnerable to disasters because of where they live. Research shows that they are more likely to occupy dangerous locations, such as floodplains, riverbanks, steep slopes, reclaimed land, and highly populated settlements of flimsy shanty homes.

Munich Reinsurance Company's annual review of natural catastrophes in 2003 said that the earthquake that devastated Bam in Iran in December of that year killed more than 40,000 people, mainly because their housing was not designed to handle a major tremor. "Traditional buildings of mud brick and heavy roofing are particularly unsafe when earthquakes strike," the report stated.

For many development strategists and critics of globalization, the vulnerability of the poor in the face of natural disasters is symptomatic of the cycle of poverty that forces poorer comm-unities (and nations) into a downward spiral of destitution. Their plight is compounded by their inability to mitigate the impacts of the disasters they suffer.

Figures compiled by the World Bank show that between 1990 and 2000, natural disasters resulted in damages constituting between 2 and 15 percent of an affected country's annual gross domestic product.

Didier J. Cherpitel, former secretary-general of the International Federation of the Red Cross and Red Crescent Societies, said in the organization's 2002 Disaster Report, "Disasters are first and foremost a major threat to development, and specifically to the development of the poorest and most marginalized people in the world— [disasters] ensure they stay poor."

Commenting on how ill-equipped poor countries are to recover from disasters, Anthony Spalton of the International Federation's Disaster Preparedness and Response Department told the Integrated Regional Information Networks (IRIN), which provides humanitarian news and analysis from Africa, Asia, and the Middle East, "Only recently have we as a sector better understood the relationship between disasters and the erosion of development gains."

Europe is not immune to the high economic cost of disasters either. The cost of environmental disasters in Europe is currently $11.4 billion a year and rising, according to the European Environment Agency's 2003 assessment.

### Preparation Is the Key to Mitigation

Investment in disaster preparedness pays. Investing in strategies to lessen the impact of disasters not only is compassionate and a government responsibility but also makes economic sense.

The World Bank and the U.S. Geological Survey estimate that economic losses worldwide from natural disasters in the 1990s could have been reduced by $280 billion if $40 billion had been invested in preventive measures. While the wisdom of hindsight is powerful, in a world of competition and scarce resources, $40 billion is no small amount to invest in preventive measures— against disasters that optimistic government officials may prefer to bet will not take place.

"Progress in the meteorological and hydro-logical sciences shows that the impacts of natural hazards can be reduced through prevention and preparedness," Michel Jarraud, secretary-general of the World Meteorological Organization, stated in March 2004. In China, for example, the World Bank estimated that the $3.15 billion spent on flood control over the past four decades of the twentieth century averted losses of about $12 billion.

Better satellite forecasting and early warn-ing systems may be partly responsible for fewer people dying from hydro-meteorological disasters. Experts on disaster risk reduction now recognize that international financial institutions, national governments, and large development agencies must accept mitigation strategies as an important part of their work.

160 However, the real key to mitigating loss of human life lies in community preparedness and education about risk reduction. "Had we invested in risk reduction before, the damage that the tsunami has done to achieving the 165 [United Nation's] Millennium Development Goals would be far less," Spalton told IRIN at the World Conference on Disaster Reduction in Kobe, Japan, in January 2005.

Salvano Briceno, head of the International 170 Strategy for Disaster Reduction, told IRIN he was optimistic about change: "The world has advanced enormously since the Yokohama conference [on disaster reduction in 1994]. There is now a high awareness of vulnerability and natural 175 disasters and the higher frequency of disasters.

"We have an increased knowledge of disasters caused by environmental degradation and global warming in particular, which is resulting in a rise in sea levels. There is no doubt that disaster 180 reduction, is more relevant; although there is more awareness, there is also more vulnerability, so it is a double-edged sword."

Despite Briceno's optimism, it remains to be seen whether international finance institutions, 185 banks, governments, and development agencies will rise to the challenges presented to them by the increasing number and severity of natural disasters. To what extent will the lessons learned from the December 2004 tsunami, and the 190 resolutions of the Kobe world conference, be implemented to reduce the pain and loss disasters cause throughout the world?

Perhaps more relevantly, questions remain concerning the estimated 2 billion people 195 affected by natural disasters in the past decade: what quality of life can they hope to recover, and will their development reduce or increase the chances of future disaster?

## 5 Comprehension Check

**Write your answers to the following questions.**

1. What has increased recently—the number of people who have died from natural disasters or the number of people affected by them? Find information in the text to support your answer.

   ........................................................................................................

   ........................................................................................................

2. What part of the world is suffering most from natural disasters?

   ........................................................................................................

3. What are three types of natural disasters? Give examples of each.

   ........................................................................................................

   ........................................................................................................

4. Why are poor people in developing countries particularly vulnerable to disasters?

   ........................................................................................................

5. What is the possible benefit of investment in disaster prevention, as suggested by the World Bank and the U.S. Geological Survey?

   ........................................................................................................

**6.** What is one example of investment in disaster prevention?

..................................................................................................................

**7.** In addition to prevention, what is the other key to reducing the effects of natural disasters, according to the passage?

..................................................................................................................

## 6  Critical Analysis: Analyzing Causes and Effects

**In small groups, discuss your answers to the following questions.**

**1.** According to the passage, what are some of the causes of the increase in natural disasters?

**2.** What effect do natural disasters have on the developing world? What is the poverty cycle?

**3.** Respond to the questions in the last paragraph. Discuss the cause-and-effect relationships between development in the developing world and future natural disasters.

## 7  Identifying Suffixes

**In "Disaster Reduction," find one example of each suffix in the chart below. Then, using the context and your knowledge of suffixes, identify the part of speech and guess the meaning of the word. The first one has been done for you.**

| Suffix | Example | Part of Speech | Word Meaning |
|---|---|---|---|
| *al* | natural | adjective | having to do with nature; coming from nature |
| *ic* | | | |
| *ity, ty* | | | |
| *ly* | | | |
| *ment* | | | |
| *ous, ious* | | | |
| *tion, ation* | | | |
| *ist* | | | |
| *able, ible* | | | |

**Scientific prefixes** are prefixes used in scientific writing. Knowing scientific prefixes can help you better understand scientific passages or passages that contain scientific words.

Here are some common scientific prefixes and their meanings:

| Prefix | Meaning |
| --- | --- |
| *bio* | having to do with life and organisms |
| *geo* | having to do with the earth, ground, or soil |
| *hydro* | having to do with water |
| *meteoro* | having to do with weather |
| *techno* | having to do with technology |

## 8  Identifying Scientific Prefixes

In "Disaster Reduction," find one example of each of the following scientific prefixes. Then, using the context and your knowledge of prefixes, guess the meaning of the word.

| Prefix | Example | Meaning |
| --- | --- | --- |
| *bio* | | |
| *geo* | | |
| *hydro* | | |
| *meteoro* | | |
| *techno* | | |

## 9  Writing a Description

Write a one-paragraph description of a situation in which you anticipated something bad happening and you did something to prevent it or prepare for it.

# Reading 3

## 1 Previewing

Preview the reading on pages 67 to 68. Look at the title. Then read the first paragraph and the last paragraph.

## 2 Scanning for Information

Scan the entire reading "Funnel Fury" on pages 67 to 68 to answer the following questions.

1. Who is a tornado expert working for the Atmospheric Environment Service?

...........................................................................................................................................................

2. Which parts of the United States make up "Tornado Alley"?

...........................................................................................................................................................

3. How many people were killed by tornadoes on the following dates?

March 18, 1925: .................................................................................................................................

April 11, 1965: ..................................................................................................................................

April 4, 1974: ....................................................................................................................................

4. Which paragraphs explain how a tornado is formed? (Give the paragraph numbers only.)

...........................................................................................................................................................

5. What is the highest estimate of tornado wind speed in the reading?

...........................................................................................................................................................

## 3 Thinking about the Topic

In small groups, discuss your answers to the following questions.

1. What do you know about tornadoes? Have you or has someone close to you ever seen a tornado or been in one?

2. Many people are fascinated by tornadoes, and some even chase them as a hobby. What is it about tornadoes that makes them so fascinating?

## 4 Making Predictions

In small groups, discuss your answers to the following questions.

1. What do you think is the main idea of "Funnel Fury"?

2. What details or examples might the author include to develop the main idea?

*Now read the text and answer the questions that follow.*

# Funnel Fury

It is the most violent event in the atmosphere. It can blow buildings to pieces, topple trains from their tracks, and send trucks and cars cartwheeling across fields. Its timing is unpredictable, its course capricious. Yet for millions of North Americans, the prospect of an encounter is a fact of life, and its appearance is a possible cause of death. It's the tornado, a violently rotating column of air that descends from a thunderstorm cloud and destroys what it touches.

Tornadoes have been recorded virtually world-wide, and their occurrence could potentially increase with climate change, says David Etkin, a tornado expert with the Atmospheric Environment Service.

Tornadoes usually occur in the late afternoon or early evening, from late winter to late summer in the United States and Canada. They are a product of the same atmospheric instability that produces thunderstorms and cloudbursts and are often triggered by the warfare between warm, moist air masses and cold, dry ones.

Still, exactly why some storm clouds produce tornadoes is unclear. To whip winds up to 250 or 300 miles (402 or 482 km) per hour is no small feat. Even for people who know tornadoes best, they remain a fascinating mystery. "It is remarkable," note storm chasers Richard Scorer and Arjen Verkaik in their book *Spacious Skies*, "that air can be made to move at such speeds over a small area."

But move it does. A weak tornado, with wind speeds as low as 40 miles (65 km) per hour, can break trees and lift the roofs off barns (thankfully, three-quarters of tornadoes are weak). A strong one, blowing at up to 200 miles (322 km) per hour, can uproot trees, move cars, and knock down houses. A violent one—and 1 in 100 tornadoes is violent—with wind speeds above 200 miles (322 km) per hour, brings total devastation. It produces the kinds of winds that lifted a 20-ton (18,143-kg) semitrailer off a highway near Plainfield, Illinois, in 1990 and bounced it more than 1,110 feet (350 meters) across a field.

Though tornado statistics anywhere can be grim, figures in other countries pale when compared to those for the United States, particularly in the densely populated area known as "Tornado Alley." Thousands have died in the stretch from Texas north through Oklahoma, Kansas, Missouri, Indiana, and neighboring states, the setting for a staggering 100 to 150 tornadoes annually. On March 18, 1925, 689 people were killed by one or more twisters, including 234 people in Murphysboro, Illinois. On April 11, 1965, tornadoes caused 271 deaths, and on April 4, 1974, 307 people were killed. Over the past few years, tornadoes have caused about a billion dollars a year in property damage.

In Tornado Alley, conditions are often just right for severe thunderstorms, which can produce heavy rain; hail; strong, straight-line winds; and, once in a while, tornadoes. Warm, moist air from the Gulf of Mexico drifts north and encounters cool, dry air from the northwest. Sometimes the moist air gets trapped below the dry air until, on a hot day, it heats up and rises, bursting through the cool air and soaring in a mighty updraft that sometimes doesn't level off until 10 or 11 miles (16 or 18 km) up. Of course, it's a lot colder at higher altitudes, so the moisture in the air condenses, causing a cloudburst or, sometimes, a hailstorm. Meanwhile, the thunderstorm clouds

produce static electricity, which in turn can
produce lightning and thunder. All in all, a pretty
wild show.

Sometimes an updraft will start to rotate due
to the same Coriolis force that causes tropical
cyclones to form and water to swirl down a
bathtub drain. Then, if conditions are right, a
large portion of the inside of a thundercloud—
sometimes a core 6 miles (10 km) wide—will
start to turn along with the updraft. It is this big
vortex—called a *mesocyclone*—that seems to
trigger smaller, tighter vortices or funnel clouds
at the base of the thundercloud. And if some
mysterious conditions are just right, one or more
of those tunnels will start to grow downward,
seemingly feeling its way like an elephant's
trunk. If it hits the earth, it's a tornado.

The funnel is usually visible because the
swirling winds surround a low-pressure core,
condensing water vapor into visible droplets.
When the funnel hits the ground, it often picks up
dirt and debris, making it yet more obvious and
ominous. A rare but reportedly striking sight is a
tornado over snow: the swirling funnel draws up
some of the snow and turns a dazzling white.

Tornadoes characteristically touch the earth
intermittently, wreaking havoc in one spot,
withdrawing into the parent cloud, and then
dipping down again elsewhere. The same cloud
may produce a series of tornadoes. The 1925
twister that killed 689 people in the United States
is thought to have been seven separate tornadoes over a 217-mile (350-km) path. The one in
1974 that killed 307 may have been scores of
tornadoes produced by the same storm system
over a 16-hour period.

The width of a tornado's path varies wildly,
from 10 feet (3 meters) up to a mile (1.6 km). Wind
speeds start at about 40 miles (65 km) per hour,
but no one is sure of the maximum because taking
a direct measurement is impossible. "By the time
a tornado is on top of your equipment, you don't
have your equipment any more," says Etkin. Some
experts think that tornado wind speeds rarely
top 250 miles (402 km) per hour. Others estimate

they could reach 300 to 375 miles (482 to 603 km)
per hour.

It is a sobering thought that global warming
could put North Americans in the path of more
tornadoes. In exploring the impact climate
change is likely to have on the frequency of
tornadoes, Etkin examined an archive assembled
by a retired meteorologist that stretched back to
1792. Etkin concluded that tornado frequency
is related to mean monthly temperatures. He
also concluded that some areas could get more
tornadoes, but that some places might get less if
climatic zones shift.

The strange stories for which tornadoes are
famous—straws driven into telephone poles,
henhouses moved but the eggs uncracked, babies
found unharmed in fields—could become even
more plentiful and remarkable. During a tornado
in Canada, a woodstove was blown out of a house
and set down upright in a neighboring field, the
fire still burning. But more often, tornadoes bring
death and devastation. As a 1987 tornado survivor
reported, "My house was sitting up against a
neighbor's house in 50 million pieces. There were
a few dead people lying in the street."

If you live in a tornado-prone area, it's good
to have a plan in case a severe thunderstorm
becomes very dark and a wall cloud drops down
from the base and begins swirling—and especially if you hear a roar like jet planes or locomotives,
or the sky turns green. Choose a safe place ahead
of time, preferably under a workbench or table
in the basement. Alternatively, seek shelter in
a small interior room, hallway, or closet. Don't
waste time trying to open windows to equalize
the pressure between inside and outside.

If you're not at home, seek shelter below
ground. Failing that, crouch down in a ditch,
depression, or culvert and protect your head
with your hands. Get out of large halls or arenas.
If you're in a car, don't try to drive to safety—you
can't outrun a tornado. Get out of the car and
move far enough away so that it can't roll on you.
If you're outside, lie in a ditch, cover your head,
and stay put.

## 5 Comprehension Check

**Write your answers to the following questions.**

1. Where can tornadoes occur? Where are they the most common?

   US and Canada usually occur in the afternoon o early evening, from late winter or late summer.

2. Explain in your own words what makes a tornado funnel visible.

   The tornado funnel is visible is when the wind is spind around embeds because of psigical force, it hits the land and dertraged eventhin aroad it.

3. Why is it difficult to measure the maximum speed of a tornado, according to Etkin?

   Because taking a direct measorgment is imposible, concaive your equipment.

4. Use your knowledge of suffixes and prefixes to explain what a _meteorologist_ is.

   The cience that deal the weather fore casting    a Person who studies the weather     marked

5. What are three examples of strange tornado stories?

   •straws driven into telephone poles, henhouses moved but the eggs un
   • kiwo a stove was blown out of a house but the fire still borning
   • My house was sitting up against a nerbar's hase in 50 milbn pieces,

6. Explain in your own words what you should do if you see a tornado and you are:

   a. In a house. → buesment
   b. Outside. → seek shelter below groun.
   c. In a car. → get out the car → lie in a dich cover your head.

   If you are in house don't open windows or doas, just find small place to stay like a closet. If you have boacment stay in there. Outside go as soon as posible a sapety place and cover you head with your hands. In the car, get out don't continue driven and do it the sarae find safety place and cover your head.

## Reading → _Understanding Chronological Order_

When describing a process or a series of historical events, writers often organize their texts according to the order in which specific steps or events occurred. This is called **chronological order**.

In paragraphs 7 and 8 of "Funnel Fury," the formation of tornadoes is described in some detail. Since a series of conditions is required for the formation of tornadoes, the author organizes the ideas in chronological order: that is, the condition that occurs first is described first, the condition that occurs second is described second, and so on.

## 6 Understanding Chronological Order

Complete the outline of the series of conditions that lead to the formation of tornadoes explained in paragraphs 7 and 8 of "Funnel Fury." Then look for and underline in the text any signal words that lead you from one step to the next.

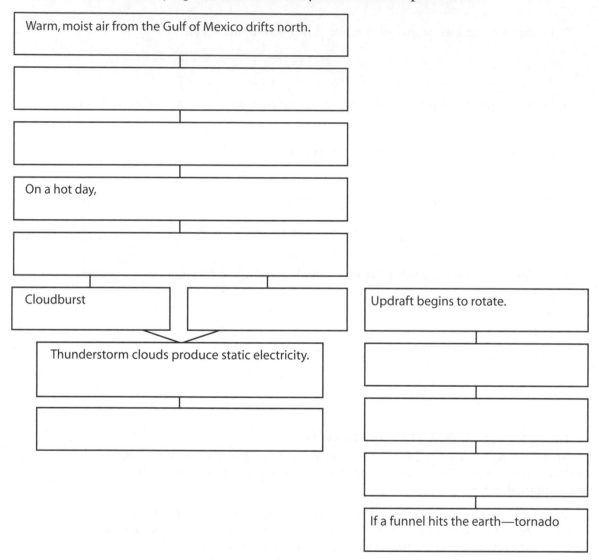

Warm, moist air from the Gulf of Mexico drifts north.

On a hot day,

Cloudburst

Thunderstorm clouds produce static electricity.

Updraft begins to rotate.

If a funnel hits the earth—tornado

## 7 Critical Analysis: Analyzing Causes and Effects

In small groups, discuss your answers to the following questions.

1. How are tornadoes categorized? Complete the chart below as you discuss this.

| Type of Tornado | Wind Speed | Percentage of All Tornadoes | Consequences |
|---|---|---|---|
| Weak tornado | | | |
| Strong tornado | | | |
| Violent tornado | | | |

2. What is the relationship between global warming and tornadoes?

## 8  Using Signal Words to Show Chronological Order

Rewrite the description you wrote for Activity 9, page 65, using signal words to show chronological order.

## 9  Vocabulary in Context

1. Find synonyms for the following words in "Funnel Fury."

    **a.** possibility (para. 1) _____

    **b.** caused (para. 3) _____

    **c.** every year (para. 6) _____

    **d.** meets (para. 7) _____

    **e.** more than one (para. 10) _____

    **f.** change (para. 12) _____

    **g.** look for (para. 14) _____

    **h.** low point (para. 15) _____

2. Complete the following sentences using the synonyms you found above. Change the form of the words, if necessary.

    **a.** All the doorways are filled with people who are _____ a dry place to wait out the storm.

    **b.** We were hoping for nice weather today, but the cold front is producing a _____ of snowstorms.

    **c.** Animal species are disappearing as a result of the _____ in climate caused by global warming.

    **d.** We didn't see the birds this year, even though they return to this spot _____.

    **e.** When people move to a new country, they _____ a new culture.

    **f.** She cannot eat chocolate because it sometimes _____ a headache.

    **g.** A _____ in an area of land is called a valley.

    **h.** The _____ of global warming is frightening many people; it seems inevitable unless we do something about it now.

## 10  Writing: Describing a Process

Based on your analysis of paragraphs 7 and 8 in Activity 6, describe the process of the formation of a tornado using your own words. Remember to use signal words to help the reader move from one step to the next.

# Writing Focus

## Thesis Statements

A **thesis statement** is a sentence that tells the reader the main idea of an essay and the writer's point of view. It can also indicate how the essay will be organized. The thesis statement usually appears at the end of the introduction, where it provides a focus for the reader before he or she reads the body of the essay.

Here are some steps to follow when writing a thesis statement.

**1. Think about the audience.** In most academic situations, the audience is the professor or another person who will mark the paper. It's important, therefore, to understand the expectations of the professor, especially those that are related to content and organization.

Some of a professor's expectations are stated explicitly in assignments. Some of them are not stated explicitly but can be inferred from the way the professor discusses the topic in class.

**2. Analyze the topic.** In some academic assignments, you are asked to show that you understand a body of information or ideas. Often, however, it's important to provide a critical analysis of information or ideas; in this case, your analysis of the topic is essential. The analysis will help you to formulate your thesis statement. Make sure you read the assignment carefully and understand what aspect of the topic you should address in your essay.

**3. Think about what you already know.** Before you write a thesis statement, consider the information and ideas that you already have; that is, what you have read or discussed in class. This can help you decide what approach to take and may generate ideas that you can use to support your point of view.

Here's an example of a thesis statement for an essay on the architect Frank Gehry:

The unique designs of Gehry's buildings, which incorporate a variety of shapes and materials, reflect both his philosophy of the modern city and his personal approach to dealing with his clients.

Supporting idea 1: Gehry's philosophy of the modern city influences his style.

Supporting idea 2: The way Gehry works with clients influences his style.

## 1   Analyzing Thesis Statements

**The following thesis statements are from student essays. Read them and, with a partner, discuss your answers to the questions that follow.**

  **a.** Impressionist art is characterized by its portrayal of everyday scenes, its attempt to capture the moment, and its innovative use of color.

  **b.** Dean Kamen's generator and water cleaner are appropriate for the developing world because they are simple, they rely on readily available materials, and they encourage entrepreneurship.

### Questions

  1. What is the point of view?

  2. What ideas will be developed in each essay?

## Describing a Process

One type of descriptive writing is **describing a process**, explaining how something happens. You saw an example of this in the passage "Funnel Fury." In a process essay, you use the same type of essay organization that you learned about in Chapter 2. However, one or more body paragraphs will be devoted to explaining how something happens. In this part of the essay, it is important to use chronological signal words, which you learned about on page 71 of this chapter, to help the reader follow the steps in the process.

Here are some ways to prepare for describing a process in an essay:

1. Think about the main causes or conditions involved in the process.

2. List the events in the order that they occur.

3. Develop a thesis statement that expresses your point of view on the topic and indicates how the process relates to it.

Here's an example of a thesis statement on global climate change:

Global climate change involves a series of steps that will have drastic consequences for people who live in coastal regions of the world.

The writer will describe the processes by which global climate change comes about.

## 2 Analyzing Process Thesis Statements

**The following thesis statements are from student essays. Read them and, with a partner, discuss your answers to the questions that follow.**

    **a.** The characteristics of the river and its surrounding landscape, along with unique weather conditions during the winter of 1996–1997, combined to make the flood of the Red River in 1997 the largest in Manitoba during that century.

    **b.** Events leading up to the crest of the Red River in Winnipeg triggered a series of powerful, personal emotions.

**Questions**

    **1.** What is the point of view?

    **2.** How does the process relate to the point of view?

## 3 Writing Assignment

**Choose one of the following topics for your essay for this chapter.**

    **1.** Choose a natural disaster. In your essay, describe the steps in the process that led to this natural disaster. Do research, if necessary. Use the signal words you learned about on page 71.

    **2.** Describe a natural disaster that affected you, someone you know, or the citizens of any country. Describe your reactions to the disaster or those of others.

## 4 Preparing to Write

**The following suggestions may help you plan and organize your paper.**

1. Brainstorm for information. List all your ideas about the topic.

2. Choose the most relevant ideas; delete any ideas that are not directly related to your topic.

3. Write your thesis statement.

4. Use a graphic organizer or an outline to plan your essay. If you choose Assignment 1, list in correct order the steps in the process that you will describe. You may want to use a flowchart like the one on page 70 of this chapter. If you choose Assignment 2, use an outline like the one on page 41 in Chapter 2. Include in it your thesis statement; your topic sentences or the main ideas of each body paragraph; and the examples, explanations, facts, or personal experiences that you will use to develop your ideas in each body paragraph. Think about how you might conclude your essay. Write notes, not complete sentences.

5. Write your first draft.

## 5 After You Write

**After you have completed the first draft of your essay, you need to revise it. The following questions will help you.**

1. Does your thesis statement express the main idea of your essay?

2. Does each paragraph focus on an idea that relates to the main idea of the essay or to the thesis statement?

3. Is each supporting idea thoroughly developed? If you described a process, are the steps easy to follow?

4. Have you used appropriate signal words?

5. Does the conclusion make a logical and clear summary statement?

## Chapter 4

# Roads to Justice

## Chapter Objectives

| | |
|---|---|
| **Reading:** | Using a Graphic Organizer to Make Comparisons |
| **Critical Analysis:** | Identifying Point of View |
| **Vocabulary:** | Identifying and Using Collocations |
| **Writing:** | Paraphrasing |
| | Writing Comparison Essays |

# Reading 1

## 1 Previewing

Preview the reading on pages 76 to 77. Look at the title. Then read the first two paragraphs and the last paragraph.

## 2 Thinking about the Topic

In small groups, discuss your answers to the following questions.

1. What are some of the reasons that people leave their home country and move to another one?

2. Imagine that you must leave your country because you are being persecuted (mistreated) for your political or religious beliefs. Where will you go? Why?

3. When people move to another country because they are being persecuted in their country, what kinds of difficulties might they encounter?

4. When people move to another country because they are being persecuted in their home country, how should they be treated, in your opinion?

## 3 Making Predictions

In small groups, discuss your answers to the following questions.

1. What do you think *sanctuary* means?

2. What do you think is the main idea of "The Road to Sanctuary"?

3. What details or examples might the author include to develop the main idea?

*Now read the text and answer the questions that follow.*

# The Road to Sanctuary

To get asylum*, immigrants must prove that they have been persecuted or fear future persecution on the basis of race, nationality, religion, political opinion, or membership in a
5  particular social group and that they can't be protected in their country. Some asylum seekers have fled countries known for corruption, brutality, and the violation of human rights. This improves their chances of getting asylum, though
10 it is not guaranteed. Of more than 500 applicants from 23 countries in 2003, those from Egypt, Ethiopia, and China were the most successful, though only about 40 percent of them received asylum. However, the situations for many others
15 are more ambiguous, such as for members of tiny religious sects in countries that are for the most part humane or for those from far-flung places in which current conditions are not well known.

Asylum seekers typically tell their story first
20 to an immigration officer, who can <u>grant</u> the request on the spot. These officers work for the U.S. Bureau of Customs and Border Protection, under the Department of Homeland Security. Nationwide, about 29 percent of asylum seekers
25 got approved at this level in 2003, according to the Bureau. Asylum seekers whose requests are not

immediately granted are referred to immigration court. Immigration judges then weigh their credibility by checking their story against what is known about the country.

Immigration lawyers and advocates say that convincing a judge is often a difficult task, and success can vary depending on which court takes up the case and whether an asylum seeker has an attorney. Nationwide, immigration judges granted asylum to only 37 percent of the 35,775 applicants, according to the Executive Office for Immigration Review. But, in the courthouse in Eloy, Arizona, the grant rate stood at 2 percent, while it was 59 percent in Orlando, Florida. Immigration judges in Chicago, Illinois, granted asylum in 31 percent of the 898 cases they heard.

Immigration courts do not provide immigrants with attorneys, and only about half show up with one. That has a considerable impact on their cases. Those with lawyers are two and a half times more likely to win their cases than those without, according to David Berten, a Chicago immigration attorney who is also a chief executive officer of www.asylumlaw.org, an information resource for asylum lawyers. Gena Lewis, a former immigration officer and now an attorney for World Relief-Chicago, said it is already too difficult to get asylum. Added to that, some immigration officers and judges have law enforcement backgrounds and tend to focus solely on preventing fraud.

Getting asylum was made trickier after September 11, 2001. Craig B. Mousin, a DePaul University professor who teaches immigration law, said judges have become more fastidious about identification issues. People are "fearful that they will let in the next terrorist," Mousin said. Omar Abdel-Rahman, a sheik whose followers bombed the World Trade Center in 1993, had applied for asylum to avoid deportation. Lawmakers in Congress used this case to push the Real ID Act, which included provisions that would make it harder to gain asylum. On February 10, 2005, the U.S. House of Representatives passed the bill. Advocates say the bill would not have had enough support in the U.S. Senate, but House Republicans later attached the provisions to a must-pass military spending bill. "We are terrified," said Oak Park attorney Larry J. Hagen, who has worked in the Chicago immigration court for more than 25 years. "Lawmakers are spreading the net so wide that they are going to hurt many people who legitimately should get asylum."

Dori Dinsmore, executive director of World Relief-Chicago, which receives federal funding to help resettle refugees, said terrorists are unlikely to exploit the asylum system. She points out that it's not easy to win an asylum bid, and the government subjects applicants to a lot of scrutiny. "It is not the way that someone would want to slip into the country," she said. "Why would you want to draw attention to yourself?" Furthermore, Fred Tsao, policy director for the Illinois Coalition for Immigrant and Refugee Rights, said many of the measures included in the Real ID Act look innocuous on the surface, "but, if you read it with an eye toward asylum-related cases, it can be pretty devastating." For example, one provision would require asylum seekers to identify the main reason they were persecuted. But Tsao said this can be difficult, as people are often persecuted for a combination of reasons, and they can't possibly know what is going on in the mind of their tormentor.

Another measure that has been proposed would give judges more discretion in determining credibility. But Tsao and other advocates say that could lead more judges to make snap decisions based perhaps on the inflection in immigrants' voices or the way they phrase things. "The way [people carry themselves] may change based on culture or on whether or not they have been tortured," Tsao said.

---

* **asylum:** status offered by one nation to a citizen of another nation, because the citizen fears harm from his or her nation

## 4 Comprehension Check

**Write your answers to the following questions.**

1. According to the passage, why do some people come to the United States to seek asylum?

   .................................................................................................................................

   .................................................................................................................................

2. What are the two processes by which asylum seekers attempt to gain asylum in the United States? (para. 2)

   .................................................................................................................................

   .................................................................................................................................

3. What are some of the difficulties associated with seeking asylum in immigration court?

   .................................................................................................................................

   .................................................................................................................................

4. Why is it particularly difficult to gain asylum in the United States right now?

   .................................................................................................................................

   .................................................................................................................................

5. What does Dori Dinsmore mean when she says that terrorists are unlikely to use the asylum system? (para. 6)

   .................................................................................................................................

   .................................................................................................................................

6. According to Fred Tsao, what's the problem with the Real ID Act?

   .................................................................................................................................

   .................................................................................................................................

## Critical Analysis ➡ *Identifying Point of View*

**Identifying point of view** is a kind of critical analysis. It helps you determine whether there is any bias, or prejudiced thinking, in what you read. It helps you better evaluate the beliefs and opinions of the author or the people quoted.

To identify point of view, look for clues regarding the credentials and affiliations—for example, job titles and/or institutions that people work for—of the author or the people quoted in the passage.

For example, in an interview about the problems that confront asylum seekers in the United States, which speaker is more likely to represent the views of asylum seekers?

- Jane Dunn, Director of Public Relations, U.S. Department of Homeland Security
- Ray Sanchez, Executive Director, Organization for Asylum-Seekers' Rights

Dunn represents a government agency, while Sanchez works for an organization that helps asylum seekers. Therefore, if you were looking for information that represents the views of asylum seekers, Sanchez's opinions might be more useful.

## 5   Critical Analysis: Identifying Point of View

**In small groups, discuss your answers to the following questions.**

1. Scan "The Road to Sanctuary" to find the credentials and/or institutions of the following people:

   Larry J. Hagen:

   ........................................................................................................................................

   Dori Dinsmore:

   ........................................................................................................................................

   Fred Tsao:

   ........................................................................................................................................

2. Is Dori Dinsmore likely or unlikely to support the Real ID Act? How do you know?

3. Is Fred Tsao in a good position to criticize the Real ID Act? How do you know?

4. If you wanted to represent the U.S. government's position on the relationship between asylum seekers and terrorism, would the views of any of the interviewees in the article be useful to you? Why or why not?

## Vocabulary Study ➡ *Identifying Collocations*

**Collocations** are groups of words that tend to appear together. Many collocations are verbs or verb phrases that tend to appear with particular nouns or noun phrases. For example, in "The Road to Sanctuary," there are several verbs that collocate with the noun *asylum*:

*grant asylum*                    *get asylum*                    *gain asylum*

It's a good idea to remember collocations as units. Knowing many collocations will improve your reading comprehension and make your writing more interesting.

## 6  Identifying Collocations

Scan the article "The Road to Sanctuary" to locate some verb + noun or pronoun collocations. Match each verb on the left with the noun or pronoun it collocates with on the right. Write the correct letter next to the verb. Note: For *g* and *h*, you'll use the same noun with two different verbs.

**Verbs**

............... 1.  flee
............... 2.  grant
............... 3.  check
............... 4.  take up
............... 5.  win
............... 6.  exploit
............... 7.  draw attention to
............... 8.  make

**Nouns and Pronouns**

a.  the system
b.  snap decisions
c.  yourself
d.  a country
e.  a request
f.  a story
g.  a case
h.  a case

## 7  Using Collocations

Write five sentences about the ideas in "The Road to Sanctuary" using some of the collocations in Activity 6.

## 8  Vocabulary in Context

For each of the underlined words in the following sentences from "The Road to Sanctuary," choose the best definition from the list on the right. Write the number of the sentence next to the correct definition.

1. Some asylum seekers have fled countries known for corruption, brutality, and the <u>violation</u> of human rights.

2. However, the situations for many others are more <u>ambiguous</u>, such as for members of tiny religious sects in countries that are for the most part humane or for those from far-flung places in which current conditions are not well known.

3. Immigration lawyers and <u>advocates</u> say that convincing a judge is often a difficult task, and success can vary depending on which court takes up the case and whether an asylum seeker has an attorney.

4. Immigration lawyers and advocates say that convincing a judge is often a difficult task, and success can <u>vary</u> depending on which court takes up the case and whether an asylum seeker has an attorney.

5. That has a <u>considerable</u> impact on their cases.

6. That has a considerable <u>impact</u> on their cases.

7. Added to that, some immigration officers and judges have law enforcement backgrounds and tend to focus <u>solely</u> on preventing fraud.

8. Another measure that has been proposed would give judges more <u>discretion</u> in determining credibility.

**Definitions**

............... **a.**  large
............... **b.**  only
............... **c.**  abuse
............... **d.**  unclear
............... **e.**  freedom
............... **f.**  influence
............... **g.**  people who speak for someone in court
............... **h.**  differ

# Reading 2

## 1 Previewing

**Preview the reading on pages 81 to 83. Look at the title. Then read the first three paragraphs and the last paragraph.**

## 2 Thinking about the Topic

**In small groups, discuss your answers to the following questions.**

1. Have you ever had something of importance stolen from you? If so, how did you feel?

2. How was the situation resolved?

3. In your opinion, what should the consequences be for a person who steals a wallet or a purse?

4. What is your definition of *justice*?

## 3 Making Predictions

**In small groups, discuss your answers to the following questions.**

1. What do you think *victim offender reconciliation* means?

2. What do you think is the main idea of "Victim Offender Reconciliation—A New Approach to Justice"?

3. What details or examples might the author include to develop the main idea?

*Now read the text and answer the questions that follow.*

# Victim Offender Reconciliation— A New Approach to Justice

One day, as Elaine walks out of the double glass doors of the mall where she works, Dave speeds by on his motorbike and grabs Elaine's purse from her shoulder. Elaine watches as her
5 money, paychecks, and ID disappear down the road. Several hours later, Dave is caught while making a purchase with one of Elaine's checks and is formally charged with a felony-status crime.

At this point, Dave and Elaine enter the criminal
10 justice system with the hopes of experiencing accountability, justice, and healing.

However, both Dave and Elaine need a process that will help them work toward understanding, responsibility, and healing. Instead of broken
15 laws and blame, true justice involves broken people and relationships that need to be repaired. Instead of inflicting pain, there is a need for healing and restitution. Crime breaks the right relationships that we are called to live in. Justice
20 is making things right.

The judge assigned to the case considers his options. Send Dave to jail and he will truly never know what exactly he has done to Elaine. Send Dave to jail and Elaine will never have the
25 opportunity to say what happened to her or to feel that she played a role in justice. The judge

postpones sentencing until Dave and Elaine have a chance to talk to each other. He refers them to the local Victim Offender Reconciliation Program (VORP).

In a meeting led by a VORP volunteer, Dave and Elaine share their stories. Dave tells Elaine that he is a missionary kid who was born and raised in Japan. His family returned to the United States several months ago. He is having a difficult time making friends and adjusting to the North American way of life. While enrolled at the local community college, he formed a friendship with another guy who lived nearby. In order to fit in and maintain this friendship, Dave had agreed to steal the purse so the two men could buy CDs and running shoes. They actually made several purchases before being caught. He admits that he knew what he did was wrong. He is embarrassed by what he did and is ready to take responsibility for it.

Elaine then has the opportunity to tell her side of the story. She tells Dave that this was the third robbery in two months. Each robbery hurt her family financially and emotionally. In fact, due to Dave's actions, the family was not able to secure a bank loan to replace some of the goods lost in the first burglary. She tells Dave that in her purse that day was her husband's first paycheck after being unemployed for more than two years. This check was now missing.

She explains her fear of walking to her car alone and of leaving her possessions unattended. She recounts her fear when he sat next to her in court. She looks him square in the eye and says, "You need to know that there is someone in this world who is terrified of you. "

Dave and Elaine talk about making amends for what happened. Elaine presents her monetary losses: the money in her wallet, the cost of replacing her identification and credit cards, the bank charges for the bad checks, and the two days of lost pay in order to attend the court proceedings.

Dave has already sold his motorbike. He also took on two jobs in order to pay her back. He pays half her losses at that time and agrees to pay the rest in one month. Dave further offers to talk with the appropriate bank personnel in order to explain that he is responsible for the actions that caused the bank loan to fall through.

Dave and Elaine talk about how things will be in the future. Elaine asks Dave if she has to worry about him doing this to her again—would he ever be waiting for her in the parking lot? Dave assures her that he wouldn't. He tells her that now that he has listened to how his actions affected her, he better understands what he has done and would never do it again to anyone. He tells her that it really affected him to hear that someone is frightened of him and that he will not forget that.

Dave and Elaine return to court for the sentencing hearing. Elaine arrives before Dave and waits for him so they can sit together in the courtroom. Dave shares with the judge what he heard from Elaine, explaining how his actions have hurt her. Elaine is then given time to talk. She tells the judge that she believes that Dave truly understands what he did and that his willingness to pay for the damages has helped her start to move on with her life. She further states that he has taken responsibility for his actions and that she has experienced justice. Dave leaves the courtroom that day with his family and Elaine, understanding what he has done and taking steps to make it right. Several weeks later, he makes the final payment to Elaine.

The criminal justice system presented Dave and Elaine with a process that would have left them both feeling alienated, excluded, and angry. Both would have continued to live in worlds of fear and pain, Dave in a world defined by punishment and Elaine in a private world of insecurity and loss. They would have walked away from the courtroom without having their needs met and without a feeling of resolution.

VORP offered Dave and Elaine the opportunity for justice that empowered them to take control of their lives and to work together to repair the damage that had been done. Their needs become the priority, leading to a greater understanding of the offense and providing the framework for resolution. VORP allowed Dave and Elaine to open themselves up in order to experience restoration, healing, and thus true justice.

## 4 Comprehension Check

**Write your answers to the following questions.**

1. Why did Elaine and Dave have to enter the criminal justice system?

......................................................................................................................................

2. In your own words, explain the purpose of VORP.

......................................................................................................................................

......................................................................................................................................

3. How does Dave take responsibility for his actions after the VORP session?

......................................................................................................................................

4. How does Elaine's involvement with VORP help her?

......................................................................................................................................

......................................................................................................................................

5. How does the author characterize the criminal justice system? (para. 11)

......................................................................................................................................

......................................................................................................................................

6. How does the author characterize VORP? (para. 12)

......................................................................................................................................

......................................................................................................................................

You used a **graphic organizer** in Chapter 2 to organize main ideas and supporting details and in Chapter 3 to show a process. Graphic organizers are also useful for making comparisons. A chart is one type of graphic organizer that is useful in making comparisons.

EXAMPLE:

| Impressionist Painting | Academic Painting |
|---|---|
| everyday scenes | scenes from history, mythology, religion |
| light, bright colors | dark colors |

## 5   Using a Graphic Organizer to Make Comparisons

Using your own words, fill in the column under "VORP" to help you remember some of the basic concepts behind VORP. (You will fill in the rest of the chart after you have completed Reading 3.)

| | VORP | Shaming Sentences |
|---|---|---|
| **Role of victim** | | |
| **Role of offender** | | |
| **Role of community** | | |
| **Procedures** | | |
| **Underlying principles** | | |

## 6   Critical Analysis: Identifying Point of View

In small groups, discuss your answers to the following questions.

1. The writer of "Victim Offender Reconciliation—A New Approach to Justice" works with VORP. To what extent does her affiliation affect the ideas presented in the passage?

2. If you wanted to get unbiased information about the criminal justice system, whom might you interview?

3. When Dave went to VORP, he had the opportunity to talk about the circumstances in his life at the time of his offense. To what extent should an offender's circumstances be considered after he or she commits a crime?

## 7 Identifying Collocations

Scan the article "Victim Offender Reconciliation—A New Approach to Justice" to locate some verb + noun collocations. Match each verb on the left with the noun it collocates with on the right. Write the correct letter next to the verb. Note: For items 4 and 5, you'll use the same verb with two different nouns.

| Verbs | Nouns |
|-------|-------|
| ........... 1. charge with | a. a purchase |
| ........... 2. form | b. a crime |
| ........... 3. inflict | c. a role |
| ........... 4. make | d. pain |
| ........... 5. make | e. a friendship |
| ........... 6. move on with | f. responsibility |
| ........... 7. play | g. amends |
| ........... 8. take | h. one's life |

## 8 Using Collocations

Write five sentences about the ideas in "Victim Offender Reconciliation—A New Approach to Justice" using some of the collocations in Activity 7.

## 9 Vocabulary in Context

For each of the underlined words in the following sentences from "Victim Offender Reconciliation—A New Approach to Justice," choose the best definition from the list on the right. Write the number of the sentence next to the correct definition.

1. He is having a difficult time making friends and adjusting to the North American way of life.

2. In fact, due to Dave's actions, the family was not able to secure a bank loan to replace some of the goods lost in the first burglary.

3. Dave assures her that he wouldn't.

4. The criminal justice system presented Dave and Elaine with a process that would have left them both feeling alienated, excluded, and angry.

5. They would have walked away from the courtroom without having their needs met and without a feeling of resolution.

6. Their needs become the priority, leading to a greater understanding of the offense and providing the framework for resolution.

7. Their needs become the priority, leading to a greater understanding of the offense and providing the framework for resolution.

8. VORP allowed Dave and Elaine to open themselves up in order to experience restoration, healing, and thus true justice.

**Definitions**

........... a. promises
........... b. most important thing
........... c. get
........... d. basis
........... e. renewal
........... f. the quality of a problem being solved
........... g. getting used to
........... h. left out

# Reading 3

## 1 Previewing

Preview the reading on pages 86 to 87. Look at the title. Then read the first paragraph and the last paragraph.

## 2 Thinking about the Topic

In small groups, discuss the following situations.

1. Two neighbors, Michael and Igor, have a disagreement about Igor's loud stereo. The stereo wakes Michael up every night and makes it difficult for him to do his job as an elementary school teacher. During the disagreement, Igor remains calm, but Michael loses his temper, and instead of discussing the situation, he punches Igor in the face, severely injuring him. In your opinion, what should be the consequences of this action?

2. A man who lied to a judge was ordered to stand in front of the courthouse and hold a sign that said, "I lied in court. Tell the truth or stand with me." What is your opinion of this punishment?

## 3 Making Predictions

In small groups, discuss your answers to the following questions.

1. What do you think *sentencing* means?

2. What do you think is the main idea of "Alternative Sentencing"?

3. What details or examples might the author include to develop the main idea?

*Now read the text and answer the questions that follow.*

# Alternative Sentencing

A farmer named Glenn Meyer could have been sentenced to two to ten years in prison when he shattered a neighbor's face for no reason, using a spare truck part. Instead, a judge sentenced Mr.
5 Meyer to probation[1]—and ordered him to post a sign in his driveway that reads: "A Violent Felon Lives Here. Travel at Your Own Risk." However, Mr. Meyer remains unrepentant and has even challenged the sign in court, arguing that the
10 judge went beyond his authority.

The sign represents an increasingly popular strategy used by judges who wish to cut imprisonment costs while shaming offenders into changing their behavior. So-called shaming
15 sentences express a deep desire on the part of society to place blame on wrongdoers. Research on the effectiveness of shaming is almost nonexistent. But scattered evidence suggests that the strategy is effective with juvenile offenders
20 who are forced to apologize in public or adults whose identities are made public in morally loaded nonviolent crimes like check kiting[2], drunken driving, or soliciting prostitutes. Even so, Mr. Meyer's steadfast resistance illustrates the
25 futility of trying to bring out shame in someone who may indeed be incapable of feeling it.

Shaming sentences have a good deal in common with strategies once used by Native American tribes or groups like the Amish, both of whom shunned members who broke societal rules. According to a recent study by University of Chicago legal scholar Dan Kahan, shaming sentences are becoming increasingly popular for a variety of crimes, including drunken driving, larceny[3], embezzlement[4], assault, burglary, illegal waste dumping, and even drug distribution. Mr. Kahan argues that the new penalties are emerging as a serious option in place of imprisonment "because they do something that conventional alternative sanctions don't do: Express appropriate moral condemnation"—and also because they free up badly needed jail space for serious offenders.

Many judges accept this logic. Some require petty offenders to wear signs or put bumper stickers on their cars noting that they have been convicted of writing bad checks or driving while intoxicated. Another form of punishment involves public contrition, in which offenders publicly state their crimes and apologize to those who were hurt.

Public condemnation is undeniably appealing. But the courts need to understand that society has gone this way before and found that the method doesn't always work. Punishments of all sorts were once administered in public as a means of deterring further crime and satisfying the need to make a public show of the offender. In the late eighteenth century, legal punishments were moved inside prison walls after societies determined that they had become mere entertainment. Early Americans turned to prisons because traditional penalties—like the stocks or public whippings—had lost the power to shame. Public disgrace lost much of its potency as cities became large enough to offer anonymity and the ties that bound citizens together loosened and then, in many places, dissolved.

Shaming is clearly useful for minor offenses, particularly those involving juveniles. It may have broader applications for more serious offenses, but judges should be cautious about using it on hardened offenders or on people for whom it will have no effect. There is probably also a need to establish sentencing guidelines. Law enforcement agencies should begin serious research into the question of when shaming sentences work and when they do not.

---

**1 probation:** a system of keeping an official check on a person who has broken the law instead of sending him or her to prison
**2 check kiting:** writing a check for money that you don't have in the bank
**3 larceny:** the crime of stealing something from somebody
**4 embezzlement:** stealing money that you are responsible for, such as in a business

## 4 Comprehension Check

**Write your answers to the following questions.**

1. What were the consequences for the man who severely injured his neighbor?

2. What other examples of shaming sentences are provided in this article?

3. According to the article, what is the principle behind shaming sentences?

4. According to the author, when are shaming sentences appropriate? When are they not appropriate?

5. What problems with shaming sentences are discussed in this article?

## 5 Using a Graphic Organizer to Make Comparisons

**Fill in the chart on page 84 with information on shaming sentences.**

## 6 Sharing Information

**In small groups, compare the chart you made on page 84. Discuss your findings and fill in any missing details. Then discuss your answers to the following questions.**

1. How are VORP and shaming sentences similar?

2. How are they different?

## 7 Critical Analysis: Identifying Point of View

**In small groups, discuss your answers to the following questions.**

1. What are Mr. Kahan's credentials? Is he in favor of alternative sentencing? (para. 3)

2. Is the author completely in favor of shaming sentences? How do you know?

3. What do you think of the punishment for the man who hurt his neighbor?

4. What is your opinion of shaming sentences?

## 8 Identifying Collocations

Scan the article "Alternative Sentencing" to locate some verb + noun collocations. Match each verb on the left with the noun it collocates with on the right. Write the correct letter next to the verb.

| Verbs | | Nouns | |
|---|---|---|---|
| .............. | 1. lose | a. | blame |
| .............. | 2. cut | b. | space |
| .............. | 3. deterring | c. | probation |
| .............. | 4. establish | d. | the need |
| .............. | 5. free up | e. | potency |
| .............. | 6. place | f. | guidelines |
| .............. | 7. satisfy | g. | crime |
| .............. | 8. sentenced to | h. | costs |

## 9 Using Collocations

Write five sentences about the ideas in "Alternative Sentencing" using some of the collocations in Activity 9.

## 10 Vocabulary in Context

For each of the underlined words in the following sentences from "Alternative Sentencing," choose the best definition from the list on the right. Write the number of the sentence next to the correct definition.

1. So-called shaming sentences express a deep desire on the part of society to place blame on wrongdoers.

2. Mr. Kahan argues that the new penalties are emerging as a serious option in place of imprisonment "because they do something that conventional alternative sanctions don't do: Express appropriate moral condemnation"...

3. Mr. Kahan argues that the new penalties are emerging as a serious option in place of imprisonment "because they do something that conventional alternative sanctions don't do: Express appropriate moral condemnation"...

4. Mr. Kahan argues that the new penalties are emerging as a serious option in place of imprisonment "because they do something that conventional alternative sanctions don't do: Express appropriate moral condemnation"...

5. Mr. Kahan argues that the new penalties are emerging as a serious option in place of imprisonment "because they do something that conventional alternative sanctions don't do: Express appropriate moral condemnation"...

6. Shaming is clearly useful for minor offenses, particularly those involving juveniles.

7. There is probably also a need to establish sentencing guidelines.

8. There is probably also a need to establish sentencing guidelines.

**Definitions**

| | |
|---|---|
| .............. | a. lesser |
| .............. | b. other |
| .............. | c. set up |
| .............. | d. appearing |
| .............. | e. standard |
| .............. | f. rules |
| .............. | g. alleged |
| .............. | h. proper |

# Writing Focus

## Writing Comparison Essays

**Comparison essays** show similarities and differences between two or more ideas or objects. Showing similarities and differences can be an effective way of making a point. One common reason for making a comparison is to show that one thing is superior to another. You can make a comparison in one or more paragraphs of an essay, or the entire essay can consist of a comparison.

A thesis statement for a comparison essay states what you are comparing, the features that you are going to compare, and whether you are going to discuss similarities or differences. A thesis statement also expresses your point of view.

Example:

As a model for attaining justice, VORP is superior to the traditional legal system because it leads to true healing for both the victim and the offender.

The point of view is that VORP is superior to the traditional legal system. The writer will probably develop this viewpoint by showing differences in how victims and offenders feel at the end of each process.

In general, there are two ways of organizing a comparison essay. These are shown below.

| **Organizational Pattern 1** | | |
| --- | --- | --- |
| Description or explanation of the features of **item 1** → | Transition to **item 2** → | Description or explanation of **item 2** (highlighting the features that are the same as or different from those of item 1) |
| **Organizational Pattern 2** | | |
| Comparison of one feature of **items 1** & **2** → | Comparison of another feature of **items 1** & **2** → | Comparison of another feature of **items 1** & **2** |

# 1   Analyzing Comparison Thesis Statements

**Analyze the thesis statements below by answering the questions that follow.**

   **a.** The VORP system of justice works better than the criminal justice system because it brings people together and promotes resolution.

   **b.** Shaming sentences are superior to the traditional legal system because they not only keep people out of prison but also allow the community a chance to express outrage at the crime.

   **c.** VORP and shaming sentences are necessary alternatives to the criminal justice system because both tend to reduce prison overcrowding while effecting behavioral changes on the part of the offender.

   **1.** What is the writer's point of view?

   **2.** What feature(s) is the writer comparing?

   **3.** Is the writer emphasizing differences or similarities?

---

## Signal Words for Showing Similarities and Differences

**Signal words** function as transitions. You read about several types of signal words on page 7 of Chapter 1. Signal words that show similarities and differences tell the reader that you are making a comparison. You use them in transitional statements that signal you are moving on to the other item in the comparison.

| To Show Differences | To Show Similarities |
| --- | --- |
| Instead of X, Y. | Just like X, Y. |
| Unlike X, Y. | Like X, Y. |
| X. However, Y. | X. Likewise, Y. |
| X. On the other hand, Y. | X. Similarly, Y. |
| X. In contrast, Y. | Both X and Y. |
| X. To compare, Y. | |

**EXAMPLE:**

There is little community involvement in the VORP process. On the other hand, with shaming sentences, the community has the opportunity to express condemnation as the offender carries out his or her sentence.

## 2　Using Signal Words for Showing Similarities and Differences

Using the chart you made on page 84, write five sentences showing similarities and differences. Use signal words.

### Paraphrasing

**Paraphrasing** is taking an idea or fact that someone else has expressed and putting it into your own words.

Paraphrasing involves revising sentence structures and using synonyms for the vocabulary in the original. An idea is not expressed in your own words if the vocabulary or sentence structure is copied from the original source. Look at the following example.

Original statement:

"If adults focus their authority on guiding children through a process of creating their own solutions to conflict, children readily learn conflict management skills of their own."

Too similar:

When adults focus on leading children through a process in which they create their own solutions to problems, children learn to manage their own conflicts.

Too similar:

Children learn conflict management skills if adults focus on guiding them through a process of creating solutions to conflict.

Correct paraphrase:

Adults can help children learn to settle their disputes themselves.

Notice how in the first two paraphrases, the writer has retained the basic sentence structure of the original. Remember, in a true paraphrase, both the vocabulary and the sentence structure should be different from those of the original.

Paraphrasing is a very important writing skill because it helps you avoid plagiarism. **Plagiarism** is taking another person's words or ideas and not giving that person credit. In other words, it is a type of theft—intellectual theft.

To avoid plagiarism when you are paraphrasing, express the ideas of the original without using any of the original words or sentence structures. You must also give the source from which you take information. The procedures for doing this will be discussed in detail in Chapter 8.

One way to paraphrase without committing plagiarism is to carefully read the original. Make sure you understand everything. Take notes *in your own words* as your read. Then put the original away. Don't look at it while you paraphrase, and use your notes only if absolutely necessary. Compare your paraphrase with the original afterwards to make sure you have not accidentally copied words or sentence structures.

NOTE: Plagiarism is a very serious offense. Ask your instructor how plagiarism is defined at your institution and what the consequences are.

### 3 Identifying Adequate Paraphrasing

Compare sentences *a* to *e* with the original excerpts from "Victim Offender Reconciliation—A New Approach to Justice" shown below. Check (✔) the sentence that has the most effective paraphrase.

1. Original excerpt: "The criminal justice system presented Dave and Elaine with a process that would have left them both feeling alienated, excluded, and angry. Both would have continued to live in worlds of fear and pain, Dave in a world defined by punishment and Elaine in a private world of insecurity and loss."

.................. **a.** The legal system presented Dave and Elaine with a process that would have left them both feeling alienated, excluded, and angry.

.................. **b.** The traditional legal system gave Dave and Elaine a process that left them feeling alienated, excluded, and angry. If they had experienced only the legal system, they both would have lived in worlds of fear and pain.

.................. **c.** If Dave and Elaine had dealt with only the traditional criminal justice system, they both would have felt isolated and angry.

.................. **d.** If Dave and Elaine had dealt with only the traditional criminal justice system, they both would have continued to live in worlds of fear and pain.

.................. **e.** After dealing with the traditional criminal justice system, Dave and Elaine were left with negative feelings. Both felt angry and isolated from their communities.

2. Original excerpt: "However, both Dave and Elaine need a process that will help them work toward understanding, responsibility, and healing. Instead of broken laws and blame, true justice involves broken people and relationships that need to be repaired."

................ **a.** In "Victim Offender Reconciliation—A New Approach to Justice," both parties needed a process that would help them work toward understanding, responsibility, and healing. Justice involves broken people and relationships that should be mended.

................ **b.** In "Victim Offender Reconciliation—A New Approach to Justice," both parties needed a process that would help them rebuild their own lives and restore the relationship that had been broken.

................ **c.** Dave and Elaine require a process that will allow them to understand, take responsibility, and heal themselves.

................ **d.** In situations in which justice has not been served, for example, in the case of Dave and Elaine, individuals need a process that allows them to understand what has happened, to take responsibility, and to heal themselves.

................ **e.** Justice involves people in pain and relationships that need to be fixed instead of a focus on broken laws and blame.

## 4 Paraphrasing

**Paraphrase the following excerpt from "Alternative Sentencing."**

"Public condemnation is undeniably appealing. But the courts need to understand that society has gone this way before and found that the method doesn't always work. Punishments of all sorts were once administered in public as a means of deterring further crime and satisfying the need to make a public show of the offender. In the late eighteenth century, legal punishments were moved inside prison walls after societies determined that they had become mere entertainment. Early Americans turned to prisons because traditional penalties—like the stocks or public whippings—had lost the power to shame."

## 5 Writing Assignment

**Choose one of the topics below for your essay for this chapter.**

1. In an essay, compare one of the approaches to justice described in this chapter with another approach to justice that you are familiar with.

2. In an essay, compare the two approaches to justice that you have read about in this chapter.

## 6 Preparing to Write

**The following suggestions may help you plan and organize your paper.**

1. Brainstorm for information. List all your ideas about the topic.

2. Choose the most relevant ideas; delete any ideas that do not connect to your topic.

3. Write your thesis statement.

4. Use a graphic organizer or an outline to plan your essay. Include in it your thesis statement; your topic sentences or the main ideas of each body paragraph; and the examples, explanations, facts, or personal experiences that you will use to develop your ideas in each body paragraph. Think about how you might conclude your essay. Write notes, not complete sentences.

5. Write your first draft.

# 7  After You Write

**After you have completed the first draft of your essay, you need to revise it. The following questions will help you.**

1. Does your thesis statement express the main idea of your essay? Does it express your point of view?

2. Does each paragraph focus on an idea that relates to the main idea of the essay or to the thesis statement?

3. Is each supporting idea developed in enough depth that your reader will understand your point?

4. Have you used appropriate signal words?

5. Are ideas from other sources adequately paraphrased? Are there any parts of your essay that might appear to be plagiarism? If so, revise those sentences by further paraphrasing them.

6. Does the conclusion make a logical and clear summary statement?

# Chapter 5

# Crossing Cultures

## Chapter Objectives

**Reading:** Taking Notes on a Reading
Understanding Proverbs
Recognizing Organizational Patterns: Cause/Effect

**Critical Analysis:** Using Empathy

**Vocabulary:** Identifying Positive and Negative Connotations

**Writing:** Recognizing Different Writing Styles
Writing Cause/Effect Essays

# Reading 1

## 1 Previewing

Preview the reading on pages 99 to 100. Look at the title. Then read the first paragraph, the last paragraph, and the headings. Scan the diagram.

## 2 Thinking about the Topic

In small groups, discuss your answers to the following questions.

1. Have you ever visited a foreign country? What were your expectations before you arrived?

2. What surprises did you encounter after you arrived?

3. How did you adapt to your new experiences?

4. What would foreigners not understand or have difficulty adapting to in your country?

## 3 Making Predictions

In small groups, discuss your answers to the following questions.

1. What do you think *culture shock* is?

2. What do you think is the main idea of "Culture Shock"?

3. What details or examples might the author include to develop the main idea?

---

### Reading ➟ *Taking Notes on a Reading*

Taking notes on a reading helps you to focus on the reading process. Taking notes as you read helps you to define the topic, note the important points and supporting details, remember the material better, and organize the main ideas in the reading.

One way to take notes is to have questions in mind as you read, look for the answers as you read, and jot down notes as you find them. You can take notes in the margin of the reading or on a separate piece of paper.

---

## 4 Taking Notes on a Reading

Use the following questions to take notes on "Culture Shock" as you read.

1. What do people have to do when they travel to another country? (para. 1)

2. What is culture shock? What are the causes and effects? (para. 2)

3. What does Pierre Casse say is important about culture shock? (para. 3)

4. Summarize Casse's four stages. (paras. 4–11)

*Now read the text and answer the questions that follow.*

# Culture Shock

Every person has a culture that has been acquired from his or her own cultural group. People tend to regard their own culture as correct and often use the standards of their own culture to judge people in other cultures. When someone travels to another country and encounters a new culture, there is an immediate need to make adjustments if he or she is to function well in that society. Problems of personal adjustment to a foreign environment are referred to as *culture shock*. Culture shock has various effects on an individual as he or she goes through its stages.

Culture shock is a common experience for a person learning a second language in a new culture. It is usually brought on by the sudden loss of familiar surroundings. The effect that culture shock has on an individual ranges from mild irritability to deep psychological panic and crisis. Culture shock is associated with feelings of estrangement, anger, hostility, indecision, frustration, unhappiness, loneliness, homesickness, and even physical illness. A person undergoing culture shock views his or her new world with resentment, and the person alternates between being angry at others for not understanding him or her and being filled with self-pity.

Cross-cultural business consultant Pierre Casse believes that individuals adjusting to a new culture pass through several stages. Casse has provided a model of these stages that summarizes the entire process. It is important to note that (a) the process is different from one individual to another and (b) people's reactions vary broadly.

Casse's four stages (see the graphic on the next page, "The Stages of Culture Shock") are as follows:

## Stage 1: First Contact

Also known as the honeymoon stage, this is the stage of happiness or euphoria due to the newness of the surroundings. According to Casse, preconceived ideas of what the new culture will be like have a tremendous impact on the way one reacts when first joining a new cultural environment. The higher the expectations, the greater chance one has to be disappointed.

Psychologists have identified these first reactions as falling on different points on a spectrum, from being excited at one end to being ill at ease at the other, with a "wait and see" position in between. Reactions depend on the individuals, their personalities, and their cultural backgrounds. Someone can be at the beginning of the joining process and become terribly upset after a while. Another individual can remain cool and just curious during the entire adjustment. In fact, one's cultural background can determine the very way in which an individual expresses excitement and uneasiness when confronted with a new culture.

## Stage 2: First Attempt to Adjust

Full-blown culture shock now emerges as the individual begins to become aware of more and more cultural differences. In this stage, the individual is deeply disenchanted and in a state of crisis. After the initial reactions, the individual makes his or her first attempt to adjust to the new cultural setting. The person is immediately confronted with three problems:

1. The person receives demands on his or her behavior from the new environment for which, to the person's amazement in most cases, he or she has no ready-made answer. The situation can indeed be embarrassing since the person does not know what to do or how to respond to new cultural situations. The solution is to change existing behavioral patterns or to create some brand-new ways of coping. This leads to the second problem.

2. The second problem is characterized by the fact that the individual's behavior does not deliver what it was intended to do. In other words, the reactions from the environment are not quite what was expected.

3. The third problem is related to the fact that the newcomer tries to observe and understand what is going on in the new social system he or she now belongs to, and it seems to the person that what other people do does not make any sense.

## Stage 3: Confrontations Creating Stress

At this stage, the person begins, slowly but surely, to accept and adjust to the differences in thinking and feeling of those around him or her. The newcomer then begins to become empathetic with people in the new culture; that is, to some extent, to view the world the way its members see it.

Emotional reactions that arise from the confrontation with a new cultural setting, while sometimes intense, are nevertheless normal. They signal to the individual the need for further action in order to survive. However, these reactions can sometimes become too extreme and lead to what psychologists call an identity problem. The individual feels very strongly the need to prove something, not only to others but also to himself or herself.

## Stage 4: Coping with Stress

In this stage, people who experience some kind of anxiety have three options to recover or control the situation. Casse characterizes these options as either dysfunctional or functional. The functional reactions include withdrawing, becoming assertive, and making adjustments. For example, in this process, the individual may decide which parts of his or her persona "work" in the new culture and which parts he or she will adjust in order to get along. Dysfunctional reactions involve fleeing from the new culture, becoming aggressive toward it, and giving up. A dysfunctional recovery, for example, may be to go home. Casse points out that the effectiveness of the options in either category is a function of the degree to which it is used. Overdone, the healthy, functional reaction becomes dysfunctional. He explains that what is good and functional for one individual may not be so for another, that the three options can be used alternatively, and that what is functional in one situation can be dysfunctional in another.

Successfully passing through Stage 4 means that the individual has, to some extent, adapted to the new culture. At this point, the individual may have renewed confidence and a degree of comfort in the culture and about the new person he or she has become.

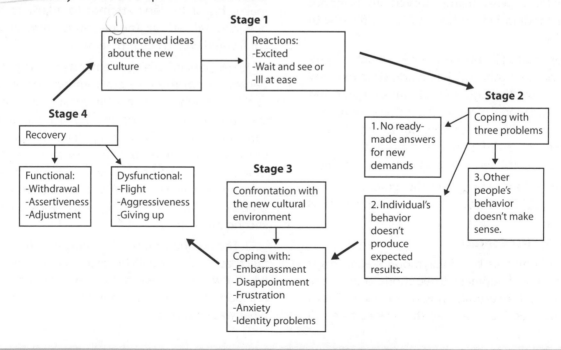

## 5  Comprehension Check

**Write your answers to the following questions**

1. Who experiences culture shock?

   ..................................................................................................................................

2. What causes culture shock?

   ..................................................................................................................................

   ..................................................................................................................................

3. List the effects of culture shock.

   ..................................................................................................................................

   ..................................................................................................................................

4. Refer to the diagram to answer the following:

   a. At what stage might a person experience an identity problem?

   ..................................................................................................................................

   b. A person behaves as he or she did in his or her country of origin, and this leads to problems. At what stage does this happen?

   ..................................................................................................................................

   c. At what stage can a person be expected to adjust in a positive or negative way?

   ..................................................................................................................................

   d. Which of Casse's stages is the honeymoon stage? Why do you think it is called that?

   ..................................................................................................................................

5. Have you experienced any of these stages of culture shock? Explain your answer.

   ..................................................................................................................................

   ..................................................................................................................................

## 6 Applying Your Knowledge

**With a partner, discuss the following situations. Decide which stage of culture shock each represents.**

1. Alvaro came to the United States to study but became so homesick he couldn't go to classes. Instead he stayed home, watched TV, and dreamed of going back to his country to be with his family and friends.

2. Suzhen finally accepted that she had to invest more time and effort in improving her English in order to excel in her graduate classes at an American university.

3. Ruth has been living in Brazil for a year and has been having a hard time trying to fit in. Today when Eduardo, her Brazilian tennis instructor, arrived at the tennis lesson once again without a tennis racket and asked to borrow hers, Ruth shouted angrily at him.

4. Nathan, an American, has just arrived in a new country for work. He's so excited about living there that he sends postcards home every day so his friends and relatives will realize what a fantastic place it is.

5. After being in the new culture for one month, Nathan invited his fellow workers to his house for a potluck dinner. He was surprised when his colleagues did not respond favorably to the invitation. Only one or two people came, but even they seemed uncomfortable, because in their country it was not customary to ask guests to bring food to a party.

### Critical Analysis ⇢ *Using Empathy*

**Using empathy** is a kind of critical analysis. Empathy is seeing a situation from another person's point of view. When you see a situation through another's eyes, you broaden your view of it. For example, one stage in Casse's culture shock process involves developing empathy with members of a new culture. At this point, an individual can see a situation from two perspectives: that of his or her culture of origin and that of the new culture. In this way, empathy is also a useful problem-solving tool.

Some people are instinctively empathetic; others can learn to be. Here are some ways to become more empathetic:

- Identify points of similarity with the other person.
- Imagine that you are the other person.
- Do an exercise in which you actually become the person. For example, a teacher might take a class to see what it's like to be a student; a doctor at a clinic might wait in the waiting room and be seen by a colleague to understand what a patient experiences.

## 7 Critical Analysis: Using Empathy

**In small groups, discuss your answers to the following questions.**

1. Review Alvaro's situation in Activity 6, item 1. How does he feel? Could you help him? If so, how?

2. Review Ruth's situation in Activity 6, item 3. What is she thinking? What might Eduardo be thinking? If you could help them, what would you do?

3. Describe a time when you were able to empathize with a person from another culture; that is, see the world or a particular situation the way that he or she saw it.

### Vocabulary ➡ *Identifying Positive and Negative Connotations*

**Connotations** are ideas or associations that words have beyond their literal meaning. Many words have positive or negative connotations. In "Culture Shock," there are many words that describe a positive or negative psychological state.

EXAMPLES:

| Positive | Negative |
|---|---|
| empathetic | panic |

## 8 Identifying Positive and Negative Connotations

**Identify the following words from "Culture Shock" as having positive or negative connotations by listing them under the correct heading in the chart.**

| accept | adapted | adjust | anxiety | cool |
|---|---|---|---|---|
| dysfunctional | estrangement | euphoria | excited | frustration |
| happiness | indecision | recovery | resentment | withdrawal |

| Positive | Negative |
|---|---|
| cool | |

## 9 Vocabulary in Context

Complete each sentence with the correct word from the box.

| adjustment | emerges | encounters | functional |
|---|---|---|---|
| impact | process | respond | undergoing |

1. When the computer was no longer ............................., Sharon decided it was time to buy a new one.

2. Moving from one culture to another can have a tremendous ............................. on a person's life. It can even affect his or her health.

3. When an individual ............................. from culture shock, he or she has a new perspective on the world.

4. Jane's been ............................. culture shock for a long time, and experiencing that kind of stress has affected her health.

5. People ............................. to stress differently: some people react positively and some react negatively.

6. According to Casse, the culture shock ............................. is a progression that involves four stages.

7. Cultural ............................. can take a long time because you often have to get used to beliefs and values that are very different from your own.

8. At first, Jack had many positive ............................. when he moved to Japan. He met several people who wanted to talk to him and show him around.

## Reading ➟ *Understanding Proverbs*

**Proverbs** are sayings that express the collected wisdom of a culture. You often encounter them in readings and conversations. Understanding American English proverbs gives you a window onto the deeply held beliefs of the culture. Because they are often based on common sense, it's usually fairly easy to guess the meanings of unfamiliar proverbs.

## 10 Understanding Proverbs

Here are some proverbs. Read them and discuss their meanings with a partner. Then add some ideas on each subject.

1. Time: Time is money.

   ......................................................................................................................

2. Absence: Absence makes the heart grow fonder.

   ......................................................................................................................

3. Friendship: A friend in need is a friend indeed.

   ......................................................................................................................

4. Taking action: A stitch in time saves nine.

   ......................................................................................................................

5. Intimacy: Three's a crowd.

   ......................................................................................................................

6. Agreements: Don't count your chickens before they're hatched.

   ......................................................................................................................

### Writing ➡ *Recognizing Different Writing Styles*

Writing can vary in terms of word choice, organization, and degree of formality. This is **writing style.** The style a writer uses matches the purpose of the passage and the writer's audience.

For example, news articles are often informal. They might have several short paragraphs, include anecdotes and direct quotes, and sometimes contain slang or idioms. Newspaper articles are written this way in order to make points quickly and succinctly and to reach audiences. This is journalistic style. Academic writing, on the other hand, is intended to inform in depth. Academic style usually features longer, more complete paragraphs that develop an idea and then support it with details, information, descriptions, or examples. Academic style also employs higher-level, more formal word choices.

## 11 Recognizing Different Writing Styles

In small groups, discuss your answers to the following questions.

1. What is the purpose of "Culture Shock"?

2. Who is the audience for the passage?

3. What kind of organization does it have? In other words, are the paragraphs written in journalistic or academic style? Give an example.

4. Is the language formal or informal? Give three examples.

5. What style of writing is used in "Culture Shock," journalistic or academic?

## 12 Writing about Causes

Read the following paragraph about Lucinda's move to the United States. Then write one paragraph in which you suggest the possible causes of her situation. Use words from the positive-negative connotations chart in Activity 8, page 103.

Just before the beginning of the school year, Lucinda and her family moved from Honduras to Texas. In Honduras, Lucinda attended a small school in a rural area. She was well-behaved and always got good grades. In Texas, Lucinda attends a large school in an urban area. Lately, she has become hostile, aggressive, and solitary. She argues with teachers, turns her work in late or not at all, and has no friends.

# Reading 2

## 1  Previewing

Preview the reading on pages 107 to 108. Look at the title. Then read the first sentence of each paragraph and the footnote. Study the pictures and captions.

## 2  Thinking about the Topic

In small groups, discuss your answers to the following questions.

1. Give an example of an incident when you did not know what was going on because of a cultural misunderstanding.

2. Describe an occasion when you tried to show respect but your action was misinterpreted and taken the wrong way.

## 3  Making Predictions

In small groups, discuss your answers to the following questions.

1. What do you think *seeing through the rules* means?

2. What do you think is the main idea of "Seeing Through the Rules"?

3. What details or examples might the author include to develop the main idea?

*Now read the text and answer the questions that follow.*

# Seeing Through the Rules

Two stories about cross-cultural interactions — one between two Native American groups, the Mohawk and the Cree, and the other between a white North American and a Native American— illustrate what can happen when people interact without understanding the differences between them.

A Mohawk band once hosted a sporting event to which they invited a group of Cree. The Mohawk, who were an agricultural people long before contact with Europeans, had developed a custom of always setting out considerably more food than their guests could consume. In this way, they demonstrated both their wealth and their generosity. The Cree, however, had a different custom. A hunter-gatherer people for whom scarcity was a daily fact, their custom involved always eating everything that was set before them. In this way they demonstrated their respect for the successful hunter and for his generosity.

Needless to say, a problem arose when these two sets of rules collided. The Cree, anxious to show respect, ate and ate until they were uncomfortably full. They considered the Mohawk something akin to gastrointestinal sadists intent on poisoning them. The Mohawk, for their part, thought the Cree ill-mannered people intent on insulting Mohawk generosity.

What is of interest in this story is not simply the collision of social customs. That might well be expected. The significant point is that each group believed that the other was intentionally being insulting and disrespectful when, in fact, each group had been making a great effort to do exactly the opposite. The problem lay in the fact that each group could only see the other through its own rules—could only interpret the behavior of others from within its own perspective.

Acts are never merely acts. They are also signals of attitude. Those signals, however, are often culture-specific. When the signal-content of a particular act is misinterpreted, it is impossible to avoid forming inaccurate interpretations of the actor's attitude. Until we understand what particular acts mean to the other, we will continually ascribe motivations and states of mind that are well off the mark. As in the Cree-Mohawk situation, the two groups or individuals will go away believing that the other was deliberately trying to insult them.

An encounter in a court of law between a Native American and a white North American offers another illustration of this. After a Native American community elder assisted in a court proceeding, a white judge went up to him, looked him straight in the eye, shook his hand, and told him in effusive terms how much he appreciated the elder's contribution to the proceedings. The judge later learned that he had made two basic errors.

First, in the elder's culture, verbal expressions of praise and gratitude are embarrassing and impolite, especially in the presence of others. The proper course is to quietly ask the person to continue making his or her contribution the next time around.

Second, looking someone straight in the eye, at least among older people in that community,

*L:* Hendrick, Chief of the Mohawks; *R:* Sitting Bull, Hunkpapa Sioux Chief

70 is a rude thing to do. It sends a signal that you consider that person to be inferior in some way. The proper way to send a signal of respect is to look down or to the side, with only occasional upward glances to indicate attention. The judge 75 had been trying to say one thing but had done so in a way that conveyed exactly the opposite. Although probably not offended, the elder most likely felt that the judge was just another of the great many white men who simply hadn't learned 80 how to behave in a civilized fashion!

In many cultures, and especially in North America, not making eye contact is considered evasive. North Americans tend to discount what a speaker says if he or she doesn't make eye 85 contact, concluding most often that the speaker is insincere and untrustworthy. This can be a particular problem in a North American court of law, where witnesses can be misunderstood simply because the judge and jury see them 90 through the lens of their own cultures, never once suspecting that the act of turning away the eyes might mean something entirely different in the witness's culture.

In his book *The Politics of Experience*, Scottish 95 psychiatrist R. D. Laing said, "Until you can see through the rules*, you can only see through the rules." We can interpret that proposition in this way: until you understand that your own culture dictates how you translate everything you see 100 and hear, you will never be able to see or hear things in any other way. The first step in coming to terms with people of another culture, then,

is to acknowledge that we constantly interpret the words and acts of others, and that we do so 105 subconsciously, but always in conformity with the way that our culture has taught us is the "proper" way. The second step involves trying to gain a conscious understanding of what those culture-specific rules might be. Until that 110 happens, it is impossible for us to admit that our interpretation of the behavior of someone from another culture might be totally erroneous.

What the two stories illustrate is that both parties in a meeting of cultures have an 115 obligation to expect difference, to expect that their interpretations of the other's words and acts are liable to be incorrect. Above all else, whenever we find ourselves beginning to draw negative conclusions from what the other has 120 said and done, we must take the time to step back and ask whether those words and acts might be open to different interpretations—whether they may have a different meaning from within that person's cultural conventions.

125 This, then, is the nature of the task at hand: learning to go beyond what we think we see and hear to ask what a person from a different culture and with a different sense of reality is truly trying to tell us.

---

\* **see through:** *See through* is both an idiom meaning "to realize that something is not what it appears" and a phrasal verb meaning "to see by means of."

## 4  Comprehension Check

**Write your answers to the following questions.**

1. Why did the Mohawk provide more food than their guests could eat?

2. In what way did the Cree show respect for the hunter?

3. What is significant about the story of the Mohawk and Cree?

4. In the second story, what were the errors that the judge made in complimenting the elder?

5. How can eye contact be misinterpreted in a North American court?

6. In your own words, write the meaning of the following sentence from paragraph 10: The first step in coming to terms with people of another culture, then, is to acknowledge that we constantly interpret the words and acts of others, and that we do so subconsciously, but always in conformity with the way that our culture has taught us is the "proper" way.

7. What does *This* refer to in the first line of the last paragraph?

8. Writers often use irony to make their point. An ironic situation is one in which what is expected to happen is very different from what actually happens. Give two examples of ironic situations in "Seeing Through the Rules." Describe how each incident is ironic.

## 5  Critical Analysis: Using Empathy

**Apply the ideas in "Seeing Through the Rules" to your own life. How do perceptions influence people's interpretations of events and issues in your life? In small groups, discuss your answers to the following questions.**

Describe an occasion when you tried to do something nice for someone but your action was misinterpreted and taken the wrong way. How did differing perceptions cause the misunderstanding? What was your perception of the issue? What was the other person's?

## 6  Identifying Positive and Negative Connotations

**Identify the following words and expressions from "Seeing Through the Rules" as having positive or negative connotations by listing them under the correct heading in the chart.**

| | | | |
|---|---|---|---|
| civilized | collision | effusive | erroneous |
| evasive | generosity | gratitude | inferior |
| off the mark | praise | sadists | scarcity |

| Positive | Negative |
|---|---|
| | *evasive* |

## 7  Vocabulary in Context

**Complete each sentence with the correct word from the box.**

| | | | |
|---|---|---|---|
| consume | contribution | conventions | illustrate |
| interpretation | misinterpreted | motivations | perspective |

1. The Mohawk served the Cree more food than they could ........................, but the Cree ate it all anyway as a sign of respect.

2. An article such as "Seeing Through the Rules" can ........................ how cultural perceptions can cause misunderstandings by showing examples from real-life situations.

3. The judge _____ the witness's body language. She mistakenly thought he was guilty because he did not make eye contact.

4. The judge's _____ of the witness's behavior was inaccurate; if she had understood correctly, she would have realized that he was showing respect.

5. Ruth did not understand the _____ behind Eduardo's actions because she did not realize that the reasons for his behavior were based on his cultural beliefs.

6. Ruth later realized that Eduardo's actions had a different meaning within his cultural _____ than they did according to the rules of her culture.

7. Thank you for your _____ to the proceedings. Your participation in the event was very helpful.

8. Tim's mother could only see the situation from her _____, but Tim's view was that he was old enough to stay out until midnight.

## 8  Recognizing Different Writing Styles

**In small groups, discuss your answers to the following questions.**

1. What is the purpose of "Seeing Through the Rules"?

2. Who is the audience for the passage?

3. Does the passage have a journalistic paragraph style or an academic paragraph style? Give an example.

4. Is the language formal or informal? Give three examples.

5. What style of writing is used in "Seeing Through the Rules"?

## 9  Identifying Causes and Effects

**In small groups, look back at "Seeing Through the Rules" and answer the following questions about how the author explains causes and effects. When you are done, discuss your answers with the class.**

1. What problem does the author identify? What are the causes and effects? (para. 3)

   Problem identified: _____

   Causes: _____

   Effects: _____

2. How does the author explain the mistake? What was the cause of the mistake, and what was the effect? (paras. 7 and 8)

   Cause: _____

   Effect: _____

## 10 Writing about Effects

Read the following description of Jane's situation. Then write one paragraph in which you predict the possible effects that may result from the situation.

Jane is a member of Culture X, In Culture X, you eat quietly. Eating noisily is considered rude and childish. You always clean your plate because if you don't, the host thinks you didn't like the food.

Jack is a member of Culture Y. In Culture Y, you slurp your food and smack your lips as you eat. This shows the host that you are enjoying the food. You never clean your plate in Culture Y, because your host might think you didn't get enough food and you're still hungry.

Jack has invited Jane to dinner at his house.

# Reading 3

## 1 Previewing

Preview the reading on pages 113 to 114. Look at the title. Then read the first few paragraphs, the last paragraph, and the headings. Study the map and caption.

## 2 Thinking about the Topic

In small groups, discuss your answers to the following questions.

1. Have you ever worked in a foreign country? If so, describe your experience.

2. When people go to a foreign country to work, what kinds of cultural issues do they face? Are the issues the same as or different from those faced by a person going to a foreign country to study? Explain your answer.

3. What do you know about life in India? Share any knowledge that you have with your partners.

## 3 Making Predictions

In small groups, discuss your answers to the following questions.

1. What do you think an *expatriate* is?

2. What do you think is the main idea of "Expatriates in India"?

3. What details or examples might the author include to develop the main idea?

*Now read the text and answer the questions that follow.*

# Expatriates in India

Bangalore, India

For the past five decades, India's best and brightest have been attracted to the glamour of the West. But today, growing numbers of Europeans and North Americans seem to be enchanted by India. Many of them are discovering exciting professional opportunities in the country's booming information technology sector. Some have fallen in love with the culture and plan to stay.

McArthur Mille, a language trainer from Canada currently living in Bangalore, says, "I was interested in working here. When there was an opportunity available, I just jumped at it. What brought me here was the kind of work that I could do here."

Sheila O'Hara first came to India from England as a tourist while still in college. Now she works with Microsoft as a language and culture trainer. "I didn't specifically ask to come here, but India is an interesting place to work if you are in the IT[1] industry, so I just took the plunge," she says. "There's a technology boom taking place. Certain parts of India are developing quickly, and it's interesting to watch these changes close up."

By far the biggest draw for recent expatriates is the information technology industry. Bangalore's reputation as a technology hub has made it the destination of choice for recent expatriates. Presently, an estimated 10,000–12,000 foreigners live or work in Bangalore alone. And nationwide, between 20,000 and 30,000 expatriates are believed to be working in India.

## Cultural Differences

Petra Klerkx, a graphics designer from Holland, says, "Life here is fast and busy. There's a lot happening in the streets, a lot of unpredictability. In Holland, what you expect, you get, which is not true here. Here life is very different. For example, people don't seem to have a sense of time here. I would even say that time does not exist. The [Hindi word] *kal* means 'yesterday' and also 'tomorrow, ' so you see it doesn't make sense!" She laughs.

Anne Julie, from France, has lived in Bangalore for a year and teaches French at the Indian Institute of Science. "I wanted to experience something different from European and American culture, so I chose India as a destination for work. In fact, India now is a fashionable place to go to," she says. Half her friends have been to India, and Indian movies and clothes are the rage in France.

## The Pluses

"Working with the Indians has been a rewarding experience," says Eric Rousseau, director of Alliance Française in Bangalore and another expat[2] from France. "The sense of family is very much present here, even in the workplace.

"In France, the individual is supreme, even in the workplace, but it is totally different here; the organization comes first," he adds.

Foreigners feel that metropolitan cities like Bangalore and Mumbai are more hospitable to them. "The day I came here, I felt at home with the large expatriate community ready to help me out with anything I wanted," says Ivan Moura, a

Swiss national pursuing his postdoctoral work at the Indian Institute of Science. "I did feel a bit intimidated by the looks of people on the streets of Malleswaram and other traditional areas where my white skin drew a lot of attention. Other than that, there has been no real culture shock."

Most expatriates enjoy the unhurried pace of work here. "There are many things that you cannot control here, like power or time. If I get caught in a traffic jam, I am invariably late for an appointment. People seem to accept this," says Moura.

"It's been like one long vacation since I arrived in Bangalore," says Moura. "The people here are nice and work happens at its own pace. There is no sense of hurrying as there is in Europe or the U.S., and I feel very comfortable here." He says he would love to stay on if he finds the right job. "There is no reason why I couldn't make Bangalore my home. The weather is great, the people are friendly and, added to this, I feel very good living here. I would love to settle down here."

**The Hassles**

The bureaucratic hassles are the biggest gripe among expatriates. "I had to struggle for five days at the Foreigners Registration office to get my work permit," says an expatriate who asked not be identified. "It makes us feel we are not welcome here."

There are also the occasional cultural conflicts. Julie Hughes, who teaches French at Alliance Française in Bangalore, says, "It gets quite difficult at times. For example, when I am having a party at 11 P.M., my landlord comes over and complains about it. It's frustrating. Otherwise, living and working with Indians is quite easy."

O'Hara's biggest criticism is the noise. "When you are at home, trying to relax, there's so much noise." She also finds it difficult to handle the cultural differences in communication. In her opinion, a lot of Indians do not communicate clearly. For example, she says, "they have trouble saying no even when what they really want to say is no." In her experience, this has led to some misunderstandings.

**The Indian Experience**

Nevertheless, most expatriates say they are enjoying life in India. There are various reasons for this.

Klerkx says, "Because I've been in Bangalore a long time, people treat me as one of them. They are accommodating. Once the first barrier is broken, things fall into place. My skin color doesn't really matter to people now."

O'Hara says, "The acceptance by people is slow but also warm. In fact, I find England weirder each time I go home."

The Indian experience is also transforming for many expatriates. Mille says India has forced him to become more assertive, as this is necessary to get along in the country.

"I didn't consider myself very nationalistic when I lived in Canada, but I now realize how much we base our identity on where we come from. I do miss my family and friends back home," Mille says.

So would they recommend India to friends back home?

"Definitely not!" retorts Martiene Meijer, a Dutch national involved with the Jung Centre." I wouldn't want to share my discovery. They must discover the treasure that India is for themselves." Alas, her little secret is increasingly dribbling out.

---

**1 IT:** the field of information technology, technology having to do with computers

**2 expat:** expatriate

## 4 Comprehension Check

**Write your answers to the following questions.**

1. What industry is "booming" in India right now, according to the article?

   ......................................................................................................................

2. To Klerkx, what aspect of Indian culture does the Hindi word *kal* illustrate? What does it say about time to her? (para. 5)

   ......................................................................................................................

   ......................................................................................................................

3. According to this article, what might be some of India's cultural values? (paras. 7–11)

   ......................................................................................................................

   ......................................................................................................................

4. What does O'Hara say about saying no in Indian culture? What kind of misunderstandings might this cause for her? (para. 14)

   ......................................................................................................................

   ......................................................................................................................

   ......................................................................................................................

5. In what stage of Casse's culture shock process are most of the interviewees in "Expatriates in India"? (paras. 15–21)

   ......................................................................................................................

## 5 Critical Analysis: Using Empathy

**In small groups, discuss your answers to the following questions.**

1. Most of the interviewees in "Expatriates in India" are from places with a higher standard of living than India's. Try to imagine their first encounters with life in a culture with a lower economic standard. What might have been different for them? How might they have felt about it?

2. What might be the value of experiencing a culture with a lower economic standard than your own? What might someone learn from this experience?

## 6  Identifying Positive and Negative Connotations

Identify the following words from "Expatriates in India" as having positive or negative connotations by listing them under the correct heading in the chart.

| booming | bureaucratic | fashionable | glamour | hassles |
|---------|--------------|-------------|---------|---------|
| hospitable | intimidated | rewarding | unhurried | weirder |

| Positive | Negative |
|----------|----------|
|          |          |

## 7  Vocabulary in Context

Complete each sentence with the correct word from the box.

| accommodating | estimated | identity | invariably |
|---------------|-----------|----------|------------|
| pursuing | sector | transforming | unpredictability |

1. There are an _____ 20,000 to 30,000 expatriates living in India, and about 10,000 to 12,000 of them live in Bangalore.

2. Jane never misses an appointment. She is _____ on time for everything.

3. At first, Rosa was just taking a few English classes, but she did so well that now she is _____ a degree in English.

4. At first, Jack found his Japanese coworkers to be very _____. They showed him around and helped him buy furniture for his apartment.

5. Newcomers often encounter a lot of _____ when adjusting to a new culture, and never knowing what to expect can be stressful.

6. At one stage of Casse's culture shock process, the individual has an _____ problem because, having made so many adjustments, the person isn't sure who he or she really is anymore.

7. Some expatriates have found that living in India has been a _____ experience: they now view themselves and the world in a very different way.

8. There are a lot of IT jobs in India right now because that _____ of the economy is booming.

## 8 Recognizing Different Writing Styles

**In small groups, discuss your answers to the following questions.**

1. What is the purpose of "Expatriates in India"?

2. Who is the audience for the passage?

3. Does it have a journalistic paragraph style or an academic paragraph style? Give an example.

4. Is the language formal or informal? Give three examples.

5. What style of writing is used in "Expatriates in India"?

## 9 Connecting Causes and Effects

**The following are some causes and effects described in "Expatriates in India." Decide which situations in the box are causes and which are effects. Then show their connections by putting them in the correct places in the graphic organizer below. One has been done for you.**

| | |
|---|---|
| -Expats enjoy life in India. | -The IT sector in India is booming. |
| -Cultural differences in communication | -Living in India |
| -Relaxed pace of work | -Some expats have experienced personality transformations. |
| -No concept of hurrying in Indian culture | -Europeans and North Americans are coming to India to work. |
| -People are accommodating. | |
| -Misunderstandings | |

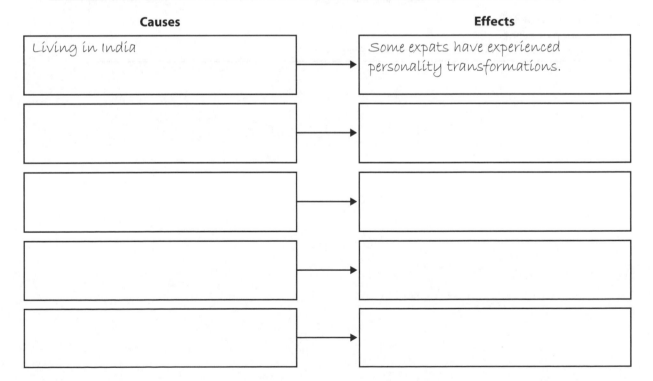

| Causes | Effects |
|---|---|
| Living in India | Some expats have experienced personality transformations. |

# Writing Focus

## Writing Cause/Effect Essays

A **cause/effect essay** has one or more body paragraphs that illustrate the causes or effects of situations and events. Showing causes and effects is one way of making an argument.

Sometimes you are describing a cause that has several effects. Other times, you are describing an effect that has several causes. Occasionally, you are describing several causes, each with its own effect. What you're describing determines the organizational pattern you choose.

| **Organizational Pattern 1** | |
| --- | --- |
| Description of situation or event (Cause) ⟶ | Effect 1 <br> Effect 2 <br> Effect 3 |

| **Organizational Pattern 2** | |
| --- | --- |
| Description of situation or event (Effect) ⟶ | Cause 1 <br> Cause 2 <br> Cause 3 |

| **Organizational Pattern 3** | |
| --- | --- |
| Description of 1st situation or event (Cause 1) ⟶ | Effect 1 |
| Description of 2nd situation or event (Cause 2) ⟶ | Effect 2 |
| Description of 3rd situation or event (Cause 3) ⟶ | Effect 3 |

## Signal Words for Showing Cause and Effect

**Signal words** function as transitions. You read about several types of signal words on page 7 of Chapter 1. Signal words for showing cause and effect help make a passage coherent by connecting ideas; when you use these words, your writing is more unified and has a logical flow from beginning to end. Signal words for showing cause and effect include the following:

*such as*
*as a result*
*consequently*
*therefore*
*so*
*because*
*since*

These expressions also show causes and effects:

| | | |
|---|---|---|
| **Cause** | *leads to* | **Effect** |
| **Cause** | *can result in* | **Effect** |
| **Effect** | *is a result of* | **Cause** |
| **Effect** | *is a consequence of* | **Cause** |

EXAMPLES:

As a result of not understanding the rules for correct table manners in a culture that was new to her, Jane unintentionally insulted her host.

Jane didn't understand the rules for correct table manners in the new culture; therefore, she insulted her host.

Not understanding the rules for correct table manners in an unfamiliar culture can lead to embarrassing situations.

## 1   Using Signal Words for Showing Cause and Effect

Using signal words for showing cause and effect, write five sentences describing the causes and effects you listed in the graphic organizer in Activity 9, page 117.

## 2   Writing Assignment

Choose one of the topics below for your essay for this chapter.

1. "Culture regulates our lives at every turn. From the time we are born until we die there is, whether we are conscious of it or not, constant pressure upon us to follow certain types of behavior that others have created for us." Clyde Kluckhohn

   Describe in what way culture affects your life. From your own culture, give examples of ways in which you are compelled to behave and what the effects are on you.

2. For most people, it is difficult to immigrate to another country. Write an essay describing the effects of immigrating to another country. Suggest what can be done to help immigrants adapt to their new home.

3. Look back at the readings on crossing cultures in this chapter. Choose the information that you think people should know before they immigrate to the country that you live in.

## 3   Preparing to Write

**The following suggestions may help you plan and organize your paper.**

1. Brainstorm for information. List all your ideas about the topic.

2. Choose the most relevant ideas; delete any ideas that do not connect to your topic.

3. Write your thesis statement.

4. For your body paragraphs, decide whether you are describing one cause that has many effects, one effect that has many causes, or several causes and effects. Using the appropriate organizational pattern (see page 118), outline the cause(s) and effect(s) that you will discuss. Write notes, not complete sentences. Think about your thesis statement and how you might conclude your essay.

5. Write your first draft.

## 4   After You Write

**Answer the following questions about your essay. Then revise it.**

1. Does your thesis statement express the main idea of your essay?

2. Does each paragraph focus on an idea that relates to the main idea of the essay or to the thesis statement?

3. Are the causes and effects clearly stated?

4. How has the information been organized?

5. Does each paragraph have a clear subject?

6. Have you used signal words to help the reader make the transition from one idea to the next?

7. Does the conclusion make a logical and clear summary statement?

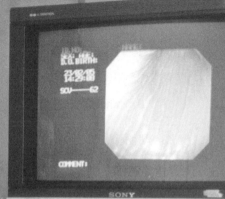

# Chapter 6

# Ethical and Social Issues

## Chapter Objectives

| | |
|---|---|
| **Reading:** | Analyzing the Structure of an Argument |
| | Mapping Information |
| **Critical Analysis:** | Evaluating Costs and Benefits |
| **Vocabulary:** | Skipping Unknown Words |
| **Writing:** | Writing Argumentative Essays |

## Reading 1

### 1 Previewing

Preview the reading on page 123. Look at the title. Then read the introduction and the last paragraph.

### 2 Thinking about the Topic

In small groups, discuss your answers to the following questions.

1. What does *moral choice* mean to you?

2. Give an example of a moral choice you have had to make.

3. What moral choices do you think athletes have to make?

### 3 Making Predictions

In small groups, discuss your answers to the following questions.

1. What does the expression *fair play* mean?

2. What do you think is the main idea of "Fair Play"?

3. What details or examples might the author include to develop the main idea?

*Now read the text and answer the questions that follow.*

# Fair Play

Whether you are an athlete on a university team, a participant in intramural or recreational sports, or someone who works out to keep in shape, you will most likely have to make some
5 ethical decisions regarding your involvement in sports. Basically, ethics has to do with moral choices that we make in our personal and professional lives—that is, deciding what is the right or wrong thing to do in the many situations
10 in which what we decide will have an effect on those around us. One of the most common decisions athletes have to face is whether or not to take performance-enhancing drugs. People take performance-enhancing drugs to reach
15 higher levels in their chosen sport. Some athletes feel that they need to take them because others athletes do; otherwise, they cannot compete at the same level. This decision is not only a concern of elite athletes. The temptation to "bulk up" is a
20 concern for the recreational weight lifter as well as those participating in many sports at all levels. What are the ethical issues involved in taking performance-enhancing drugs? *unethical*

When you take performance-enhancing drugs,
25 you hurt yourself as well as others. First, there are the health risks. If the drugs you take are dangerous to your health and you suffer physical harm from taking them, then you are hurting those who care for you. Also, if you play sports at
30 a high level and are caught taking a drug that is banned in your sport, you could suffer fairly severe penalties that will hurt you as well as the people who have supported you in your involvement in the sport. Finally, not only will you hurt your fam-
35 ily and friends by taking performance-enhancing drugs, but you will also hurt your competitors. If you do drugs and your competitors don't, an element of unfairness has been added to the game. Furthermore, they may feel coerced into
40 taking drugs in order to compete with you.

Taking performance-enhancing drugs damages the spirit of sports and competition. Sport is often perceived as an opportunity to test one's abilities against people with similar skills. If
45 someone plays simply to win, it might be difficult to persuade him or her that performance-enhancing drugs are unethical. However, if you participate in sports to improve your skills, there is a good reason not to take performance-
50 enhancing drugs—these drugs do not improve your skill level. They may increase your strength and speed, but they will not improve your technique. Don't get me wrong—with the added strength and/or speed, you may increase your
55 chances of winning. However, that does not mean that you are the more skilled player.

Playing "drugged" changes the nature of athletic competition. According to R. Simon in *Fair Play: Sports, Values & Society*, "[T]he whole
60 point of athletic competition is to test the athletic ability of persons, not the way bodies react to drugs." Thus, I would argue that if society wants sports to remain a competition between people as an end in itself, not a means to achieve the
65 goal of winning, people should refrain from using performance-enhancing drugs. Furthermore, keeping the playing field even is a test not just of athletic ability but also of ethical standards.

## 4  Comprehension Check

**Write your answers to the following questions.**

1. Explain in your own words the meaning of *ethics*.

   *Made decisions always keeping in mind what is good and what is bad and why. Also the consequences*

2. According to the passage, what is one of the most important ethical decisions an athlete has to make?

   *Wether or not to take performance-enhancing drugs.*

3. In paragraph 2, the author says that "they may feel coerced into taking drugs." What is a synonym for *coerced*? To whom does *they* refer?

   *To force / beset, bully, concuss, constrain oblige, repress*

4. What effect does taking illegal drugs have on the personal and professional life of an athlete?

   *• The health risk.        1 • hurt family and friends.*
   *• Penalties.        1 • coerced your competitor to take drugs.*

5. How is it possible to "hurt" the sport? What is a synonym for *hurt* as used in this reading?

   *If you don't play by the rules you are not showing respect for the sport. Hurt: damage, dishonor.*

## 5   Analyzing the Structure of a Reading

Complete the chart below. First, decide what the thesis statement of "Fair Play" is. In other words, what is the author trying to persuade us to think? Then write short answers to the questions about the structure of "Fair Play." Finally, decide whether each paragraph supports the pro or con side of the issues raised in the thesis statement.

| | Pro or Con? |
|---|---|
| **Thesis Statement:** _to take performance -enhancing drugs for athlete people is negative for them because them ethica can be readable questionable the consequences in/a personal and public life can be huge and really bad and finally, the sport looks in negative way._ | |
| **Paragraph 1: What ethical issue in sports is the subject of this passage?** <br><br> **Answer:** _the athletes wetter or not take performance—enhancing drugs._ | Pro: They have the abilities to take the best desition. <br> Con: A lot of people do it & looks easy. |
| **Paragraph 2: What are the effects of taking drugs?** <br><br> **Answer:** _The healt risk. Hurt family and friends. Penalties._ | Po: — <br> Con: Everithing. |
| **Paragraph 3: What are the effects of taking drugs on the practice of sports?** <br><br> **Answer:** _•Coerced your competitor to take drugs •They may increase your strength and speed, but they will not improve your technique._ | Pro: — <br> con: everithing. |
| **Paragraph 4: What does the author conclude?** <br><br> **Answer:** _•Playing "drugged" changes the nature of athletic competition •keeping the playing field even U a test not just of athletic ability but also of ethical standards._ | Pro |

Now compare charts with a partner. Discuss your answers to the following questions.

What is the author's position on this topic? Has the author supported his or her thesis statement well in the body paragraphs? If yes, how does the author do it?

## Critical Analysis ➟ *Evaluating Costs and Benefits*

**Evaluating costs and benefits** is a kind of critical analysis. It involves seeing the advantages and disadvantages of a situation or issue. It is useful in developing arguments and in solving problems. It is especially useful in making ethical decisions.

To evaluate costs and benefits, ask yourself: What will be gained from this decision? What will be lost as a result of making this decision?

One way to evaluate the costs and benefits of a situation or an issue is to create a chart like the following and to list all the possibilities in each section.

| Costs | Benefits |
|-------|----------|
|       |          |

## 6  Critical Analysis: Evaluating Costs and Benefits

**Read the scenario. Then, use a chart like the one in the box above to help you decide what you would do. In small groups, discuss the following questions.**

Imagine that you are a talented athlete whose dream is to compete in the Olympics. Your family also relies on you to support them financially.

You have just signed up with a coach who has a reputation for being able to take athletes to the Olympic Games. After observing you perform, the coach tells you that if you want to be ready for the Olympics, you will need to improve your performance by a large degree in a very short time. Athletes on your own team and other people tell you that you should take performance-enhancing drugs.

1. What would you do? Why?

2. What are the costs and benefits of your decision?

## 7 Vocabulary in Context

Find the following sports- and drug-related collocations in the passage. Study them in context and guess their meanings. Write your guesses on the lines.

works out (para. 1): ................................................................................
................................................................................

keep in shape (para. 1): ................................................................................
................................................................................

bulk up (para. 1): ................................................................................
................................................................................

do drugs (para. 2): ................................................................................
................................................................................

test one's abilities (para. 3): ................................................................................
................................................................................

plays to win (para. 3): ................................................................................
................................................................................

achieve the goal (para. 4): ................................................................................
................................................................................

## 8 Using Collocations

Complete each sentence with the correct form of one of the collocations in the list above.

1. Cheating will not help you ............................ you set for yourself in life; if you want to succeed, you have to play fair.

2. Jane participates in competitive tennis because she enjoys having the opportunity to ............................ against those of the other participants.

3. Jane rarely loses. When she plays tennis, she ............................ .

4. Jane ............................ in the gym every morning with a trainer who instructs her in the best ways to exercise.

5. ............................ means adding muscle mass to the body.

6. Jack decided to take steroids in order to add muscle to his body quickly. It's unfortunate that instead of developing his muscles the natural way, he chose to ............................ .

7. Most experts agree that the best way to ............................ is to exercise regularly and not overeat.

### 9 Identifying Arguments

Use the chart below to list as many arguments as you can on both sides of the issue of using performance-enhancing drugs. Refer to the reading and to the critical analysis activity you did on page 126.

| Using Performance-Enhancing Drugs | |
|---|---|
| Pro | Con |
| | |

### 10 Writing

Write a paragraph giving your opinion of performance-enhancing drugs. Use some of the sports- and drug-related collocations you have learned. Be sure to support your opinion.

## Reading 2

### 1 Previewing

Preview the reading on pages 129 to 130. Look at the title. Then read the first four paragraphs, the last paragraph, and the headings.

### 2 Thinking about the Topic

In small groups, discuss your answers to the following questions.

1. What is the purpose of hospital emergency rooms (ERs)? Why do people use them? What are some of the more serious medical conditions that people have when they are sent to an emergency room?

2. Have you ever been to an ER? If so, explain what happened.

3. Has anyone in your family ever had a serious, life-threatening medical condition? If so, to what extent did you and other family members become involved in that person's medical care?

### 3  Making Predictions

**In small groups, discuss your answers to the following questions.**

1. What do you think is the main idea of "Being There"?

2. What details or examples might the author include to develop the main idea?

*Now read the text and answer the questions that follow.*

# Being There

Patients are becoming increasingly knowledgeable about their own medical care, and as a result, both patients and their family members are becoming more involved in medical decision making. For example, family members are increasingly present during life-and-death emergency room procedures and often have to make serious ethical decisions such as whether to continue life support or resuscitate a critically ill relative.

Should family members be spared the agony of watching critically ill relatives suffer? Or is family presence during medical practices a basic human right? What are the pros and cons of family presence during invasive medical procedures?

Family presence during cardiopulmonary resuscitation (CPR) and invasive procedures has been a topic of debate in recent years, but appears to be associated with beneficial outcomes for both family members and patients, according to research conducted by Cathie Guzzetta, RN, PhD.

Dr. Guzzetta first became involved in family presence research when she was employed as a research consultant at a hospital in Dallas, Texas. A nurse at the hospital asked Guzzetta, "Why do we ban all families from the bedside during CPR?" after nearly losing her job for allowing a couple to be present during the resuscitation of their 14-year-old son. "I said, 'I really don't have an answer for that,'" recalled Dr. Guzzetta.

### Support for Family Presence

Shortly after Guzzetta's experience, several organizations—including the American Heart Association (AHA) and the American Association of Critical Care Nurses—issued guidelines supporting family presence. Additionally, family presence recommendations have been incorporated into curricula for several emergency care training programs.

According to Dr. Guzzetta, all of the organizations recommend that a designated family facilitator—a nurse, chaplain, social worker, or child life specialist who is familiar with family presence guidelines and trained in crisis management—be involved to assist the family throughout the event. The family facilitator assesses the family to rule out possible combative behavior, emotional instability, or behaviors consistent with an altered mental state. If family members are judged as suitable candidates for family presence, and if a supervising physician or nurse agrees, the family is offered the option of being present during the emergency procedure. If the family members accept, they are escorted into the room by the family facilitator, who then finds a place for them to stand or sit, encourages them to support the patient, and stays with the family.

### Fears Associated with Family Presence

Various surveys have been conducted in recent years to evaluate health care providers' feelings about family presence during emergency procedures. Most notable was a study published by Helmer et al. The study asked, "How do you feel about bringing families in?" Results indicated that most respondents considered family presence inappropriate during all phases of resuscitation and invasive procedures. Other studies had similar results. One survey that was conducted at 81 Arkansas hospitals revealed that only 38 percent of the medical professionals would consider allowing family presence during CPR.

Dr. Guzzetta said the most frequently documented concern is that family members will become too emotional and will interfere with patient care. "This concern is the number one legitimate argument against family presence. No one wants any interruption in patient care."

Other concerns, she said, include staffing shortages and high patient volumes, risk of litigation, interference with resident training, violation of patient confidentiality, and interference with resuscitation attempts. "To date, there is no research evidence that documents support for any of these fears," said Dr. Guzzetta.

## Positive Outcomes for Families and Patients

When discussing the outcomes of actual family presence events, Guzzetta refers to a study done several years ago at a hospital in Michigan, in which eighteen families whose loved ones had died in the emergency department were asked if they would have chosen to be present, if given the option. Seventy-two percent of family members said they would have wanted the option. In response to this finding, the hospital created a family presence program, and 30 events were evaluated. The findings suggested that family presence was associated with positive outcomes and no interruption in patient care.

Dr. Guzzetta noted that because of low survival rates following CPR, it has been difficult to assess patients' opinions about family presence. Despite this obstacle, Guzzetta published, in collaboration with several colleagues, findings

of patient, family, and health care provider perceptions of family presence during CPR or invasive procedures. Patients reported that they felt family presence comforted them, provided help, and served to remind providers of the patient's personhood. Family members reported feeling as though they had been given an active role in the care of their loved one when allowed to be present. This role may have been as simple as sitting on one side of the room and praying for the patient, encouraging the patient, singing to the patient, or touching the patient. Family members also reported that being present during emergency procedures removed doubt about what was happening to their loved one and reduced their anxiety and fears. "They could see that everything possible was being done," she said. Health care providers involved in these events reported that family members provided emotional support, translated for the patient, and furnished essential patient information.

## Written Policies on Family Presence

Dr. Guzzetta emphasized the importance of establishing written family presence policies in all critical care units and emergency departments. A survey of 1,000 critical care and emergency nurses conducted in 2003 revealed that 95 percent of respondents worked in critical care units and emergency departments with no written family presence policies. "Because of the consistent body of evidence documenting the beneficial effects of family presence, we need to be working with physicians and administrators and organizations to adopt evidence-based practice guidelines for the option of family presence during CPR and invasive procedures," she concluded.

## 4 Comprehension Check

**Write your answers to the following questions.**

1. Explain in your own words what "family presence during cardiopulmonary resuscitation (CPR) and invasive procedures" means. (para. 3)

   *The person of the parent can stay inside the emergency room (and can opinion to in acritical moments)*

2. How did Dr. Guzzetta become interested in the issue of family presence?

   *Was in Dallas during the process resuscitation of one 14 year old gug, who can have him parents in the emergency room*

3. What procedures do the AHA and other medical organizations recommend for family presence?

   *Nurse, chaplain, social worker or child life specialist who is familiar with family presence guidelines and trained in crisis management*

4. How do health care providers feel about family presence, in general?

   *Considered family presence inappropriate during all phases or (CPR)*

5. In general, how do family members feel about family presence?

   *Positive outcomes*

6. Has Guzzetta been able to assess patients' feelings about family presence? Why or why not?

   *Patients don't after survive in the situations.*

7. What does Guzzetta recommend in the final paragraph?

   *Establish the policies in all critical care centers and emergency departments*

## 5 Critical Analysis: Evaluating Costs and Benefits

**Read the scenario. Use a chart like the one on page 126 to help you make the decision. In small groups, discuss the following questions.**

Imagine that your grandfather has been rushed to the emergency room after a having a heart attack. You and other family members arrive shortly after he has been admitted. The health care providers are in the process of trying to resuscitate him. They will allow you to be present during this procedure.

1. What are the benefits for you and your family members of being present?

2. What are the benefits for your grandfather? What are the costs (that is, the emotional costs)?

3. What will you do? Give reasons for your decision.

## 6 Vocabulary in Context

**The following sentences are from the reading passage. From the context, guess the meaning of each underlined word or phrase and then give a synonym for it. If you cannot provide a one- or two-word synonym, rewrite the sentence without the underlined word or phrase in a way that explains its meaning. Be careful not to change the meaning of the original sentence.**

1. The family facilitator <u>assesses</u> the family to rule out possible combative behavior, emotional instability, or behaviors <u>consistent with</u> an altered mental state.

   assesses: ................................................................................................................................

   consistent with: ....................................................................................................................

2. Family presence during cardiopulmonary resuscitation (CPR) and invasive procedures has been a topic of <u>debate</u> in recent years, but appears to be associated with <u>beneficial</u> outcomes for both family members and patients, according to research conducted by Cathie Guzzetta, RN, PhD.

   debate: ..................................................................................................................................

   beneficial: .............................................................................................................................

3. Dr. Guzzetta said the most frequently <u>documented</u> concern is that family members will become too emotional and will interfere with patient care.

   ................................................................................................................................................

4. Dr. Guzzetta emphasized the importance of <u>establishing</u> written family presence policies in all critical care units and emergency departments.

   ................................................................................................................................................

5. Despite this obstacle, Guzzetta published, in collaboration with several <u>colleagues</u>, findings of patient, family, and health care provider <u>perceptions</u> of family presence during CPR or invasive procedures.

   colleagues: ............................................................................................................................

   perceptions: ..........................................................................................................................

## Reading ⇒ *Mapping Information*

**Mapping information** is showing the relationships among ideas in a visual format. It is a map of the concepts, ideas, and supporting information. For example, you can show the relationship between the topic of a reading and the ideas that are related to it. You can also show how a reading passage is organized and how ideas are connected. You can use various kinds of graphic organizers to map the information in a reading. You have seen some of these in Chapters 2 and 4.

## 7  Mapping Information

**First, discuss with a partner your answers to the following questions.**

1. What is the purpose of the first four paragraphs?

2. What is the issue?

3. Where is the thesis statement? What is it?

4. What side of the issue does the author take?

5. What is the purpose of paragraphs 5–6? In other words, how might background on procedures for family presence help the author's argument?

6. What side of the issue does the author present in paragraphs 7–9? What might be the reason for this? What kind of information supports this side of the issue?

7. What side of the issue does the author present in paragraphs 10–11? What kind of information supports this side of the issue?

8. What is the purpose of paragraph 12?

**Now, map "Being There" to show the arguments for and against the issue of family presence. Use the information from the questions above to outline the passage using the graphic organizer below.**

| Paragraphs 1–4: Introduction |
|---|
| Purpose:_____<br>Issue:_____<br>Thesis:_____<br>_____ |

↓

| Paragraphs 5–6: Background |
|---|
| Purpose:_____<br>Support:_____<br>_____ |

↓

| Paragraphs 7–9: Con |
|---|
| Purpose:_____<br>Support:_____<br>_____ |

↓

| Paragraphs 10–11: Pro |
|---|
| Purpose:_____<br>Support:_____<br>_____ |

↓

| Paragraph 12: Conclusion |
|---|
| Purpose:_____<br>Support:_____<br>_____ |

## 8  Writing a Summary

Write a summary of the arguments on both sides of the family presence issue presented in "Being There." Refer to the map you made in Activity 7.

# Reading 3

## 1  Previewing

Preview the reading on pages 135 to 136. Look at the title. Then read the first few paragraphs and the last paragraph.

## 2  Thinking about the Topic

In small groups, discuss your answers to the following questions.

1. What are some moral decisions that doctors have to make?

2. How do you think doctors learn to do the complicated medical procedures they have to perform?

3. What is your opinion of doctors practicing on animals? Give reasons for your answer.

4. Do you think it is proper for medical students to practice on human beings? Give reasons for your answer.

## 3  Making Predictions

In small groups, discuss your answers to the following questions.

1. What do you think *ghastly* means?

2. What do you think is the main idea of "Medical Ethics: A Ghastly Way to Practice"?

3. What details or examples might the author include to develop the main idea?

*Now read the text and answer the questions that follow.*

# Medical Ethics: A Ghastly Way to Practice

Dr. Christine Meyers, a young emergency medicine resident at Montreal General Hospital, saw opportunity in death. She was a member of a trauma team that had tried and failed to revive an
5 elderly surgical patient. As soon as he died, she called over a medical student and together they began a central-line insertion into a large blood vessel in the man's upper chest.

This is a last-ditch procedure normally reserved
10 for trauma victims on the brink of death. But in this instance, the medical student and Dr. Meyers were the only ones to benefit: they got a chance to practice a difficult procedure on someone who couldn't be injured by a mistake.

15 Not everyone felt that their medical education trumped the fact that they were messing about with a dead person without permission. A veteran nurse walked in on them and objected.

"'Don't you realize the patient is dead?'" Dr.
20 Meyers recalls her saying. "I said, 'I think it's better for the medical student to learn this procedure on someone who can't be harmed rather than doing it for the first time on a patient who is alive.' The nurse felt what I was doing was inherently
25 disrespectful.'"

The nurse reported the incident to the hospital's ethics board. A hearing was held, and the board decided that Dr. Meyers's action was inappropriate. "The non-physician members of
30 the board were pretty outraged," she recalls.

Dr. Meyers was in one of the gray areas of medical ethics. How does a resident learn without practicing? How do you teach someone the hundreds of lifesaving techniques used in an
35 emergency department?

Dr. Meyers and many others believe that acquiring experience by practicing on the newly dead—before they've become rigid with rigor mortis—is the best way to spare future patients
40 the mistakes of insufficiently prepared doctors.

But every dead body is someone's mother, father, offspring, or sibling. It can be daunting for young residents to get consent from families for such procedures.

45 This issue has been debated in bioethics journals for years. Is it the best way for students to learn? Should hospitals have policies? Should family consent be required? There are no easy answers.

50 What has evolved in the absence of a national protocol in the United States and Canada is passive acceptance—a belief that families would agree if we asked them, so why bother them while they are grieving? A 1989 survey of 919 U.S. hospitals
55 found that 54 percent had practiced on the newly dead and just 3 percent of those hospitals had a policy requiring family consent.

Clinical ethicist Dr. Eugene Bereza of the Royal Victoria Hospital says he was appalled when he
60 learned of the Meyers incident. "Doctors don't have a monopoly on making these decisions," he says. "Society never said to the medical profession, 'Forget about what we think.' Society never said, 'On issues that society is really uptight about, go
65 ahead and disregard us.'"

Dr. Pat Melanson, an emergency and critical care specialist, says he has never practiced on the newly dead, but he's seen it done several times. A teaching doctor at McGill Medical School, Dr.
70 Melanson says he thinks it's probably a good way to learn. But the consent issue is tricky. "It would be useful, strictly from the point of view of overall benefit, to allow residents to perform these skills on the newly dead. I think there are other ways
75 to do it, but I'm not sure they're ideal. On the other hand, I do find the procedure somewhat distasteful."

In a very informal survey, Dr. Meyers polled 32 emergency department physicians and found
80 that more than 60 percent admitted to practicing on newly dead people. Only 3 percent had acquired family consent; most felt it was wrong not to.

It isn't just emergency residents who are affected. Veteran physicians also need to practice seldom-used skills.

For example, emergency medicine physicians should be proficient at hundreds of lifesaving techniques, including open-heart massages, central-line insertions, and alternate forms of ventilation, including cricothyroidotomy, in which a tube is inserted into the trachea via a hole in the neck. Dr. Meyers hasn't done any of these procedures in her three years of training. Someday, she says, she could be called upon to use those skills.

Even Dr. Melanson is concerned about his skills, long ago honed in the cadaver lab and the intensive care unit. "I've done many cricothyroidotomies but I haven't done one in three years. So the next time I have to do one, will I have the level of confidence I had before?"

Dr. Kenneth Iserson, an Arizona surgeon who's written extensively in support of practicing on the newly dead, argues there is an ethical imperative because it provides the best training ground. He says society, by seeking perfection in its doctors, has implicitly given its consent.

If the autonomy of the dead is so important, asks Dr. Meyers, what about the rights of the living? Anytime a person is anesthetized for surgery, he or she runs a risk of having the intubation done by a medical student who has never done it before.

And sometimes, doctors keep patients alive in order to practice resuscitation techniques. Doctors who spoke of this said it's hard to judge sometimes whether resuscitation is done for the sake of experience or whether it is a resident's final desperate attempt to save a life.

These are all practices that blur the informed-consent and autonomy rules that guide doctors. "My position is that it shouldn't be done surreptitiously," says Dr. Melanson. "It should be out in the open. And if the resident has discomfort approaching the family, then I think that tells you something about how much they think the benefit will be."

So what are the alternatives? When Dr. Melanson took an advanced trauma life-support course ten years ago, students used animals that had been killed for the sole purpose of being practiced on. Animal rights activists have effectively eliminated that avenue. These days, his students use pig tracheas, leftovers from the local butcher. But pig and human throats aren't identical.

During his training, Dr. Bereza recalls an excruciating two hours during which he and a classmate practiced IV insertion on each other.

Paying volunteers is another option, but that has drawbacks. Some techniques are simply too painful and mutilating.

Doctors can visit a cadaver lab, but tissue changes soon after death.

Virtual cadavers are one possible alternative, where users look at a computer screen while working on a model—but most experts agree that this isn't a good substitute for hands-on training.

Dr. Bereza says he understands the need for training, but he vehemently opposes any action without family consent. "You'd be surprised at how many people are willing when approached properly," he says.

## 4 Comprehension Check

**Write your answers to the following questions.**

1. In paragraph 2, you read that "they got a chance to practice a difficult procedure on someone who couldn't be injured by a mistake." Who are *they*? What procedure was practiced?

   ............................................................................................................................

2. Why did the nurse report the case to the ethics board?

   ............................................................................................................................

   ............................................................................................................................

3. What is the ethical issue in this passage?

   ............................................................................................................................

   ............................................................................................................................

4. What policy do most hospitals have regarding practicing on newly deceased patients?

   ............................................................................................................................

5. Does Dr. Bereza agree with Dr. Meyers? Give support for your answer.

   ............................................................................................................................

   ............................................................................................................................

6. Why do so many doctors practice on newly dead people without the consent of the deceased people's relatives?

   ............................................................................................................................

   ............................................................................................................................

## 5 Critical Analysis: Evaluating Costs and Benefits

**In small groups, discuss your answers to the following questions.**

Should family consent always be required if a hospital wants medical students to practice on a body just after death? Or are the benefits of practicing on the newly dead so significant that family consent is irrelevant? Give reasons for your answers.

## Vocabulary ➡ *Skipping Unknown Words*

You can often **skip unknown words** and expressions when you read. This is because you don't have to know the meaning of every word or expression in a reading in order to understand the general meaning of the whole reading. You need to know enough words to understand the main idea and the supporting ideas and to understand how supporting information connects to the main idea, but this doesn't require knowing every word.

For example, in "Medical Ethics: A Ghastly Way to Practice," there are some medical and scientific terms. Do you need to know all of them in order to understand the passage? No. For example, in paragraph 1, you may not know what a central-line insertion is, but from the context, you know that it's a medical procedure, and that's all you need to know to understand the sentence.

Here are some steps to follow when you encounter an unknown word or phrase:

Step 1: Ask yourself whether you need to know it in order to understand the main idea and supporting information in the passage. If the answer is no, skip it and continue reading. It the answer is yes, go to Step 2.

Step 2: Ask yourself whether you can guess the meaning from context. If the answer is yes, guess and continue reading. If the answer is no, go to Step 3.

Step 3: Look the word up in a dictionary or ask someone.

## 6 Skipping Unknown Words

**Find the following sentences from "Medical Ethics: A Ghastly Way to Practice" in context. Decide whether you can skip each underlined term and still understand the important ideas in the passage. If you can't skip a term, see if you can guess the meaning from the context. If you need to look up the term, give a definition.**

1. Dr. Meyers and many others believe that acquiring experience by practicing on the newly dead—before they've become rigid with <u>rigor mortis</u>—is the best way to spare future patients the mistakes of insufficiently prepared doctors.

   ☐ Skip          ☐ Guess: .............................          ☐ Look up

   **Definition:** ...........................................................................

2. For example, emergency medicine physicians should be proficient at hundreds of lifesaving techniques, including open-heart massages, central-line insertions, and alternate forms of ventilation, including <u>cricothyroidotomy</u>, in which a tube is inserted into the trachea via a hole in the neck.

   ☐ Skip          ☐ Guess: .............................          ☐ Look up

   **Definition:** ...........................................................................

3. Even Dr. Melanson is concerned about his skills, long ago honed in the <u>cadaver</u> lab and the intensive care unit.

   ☐ Skip          ☐ Guess: .............................          ☐ Look up

   **Definition:** ...........................................................................

4. These are all practices that blur the informed-consent and autonomy rules that guide doctors. "My position is that it shouldn't be done surreptitiously," says Dr. Melanson.

☐ Skip    ☐ Guess: _____    ☐ Look up

**Definition:** _____

5. These days, his students use pig tracheas, leftovers from the local butcher. But pig and human throats aren't identical.

☐ Skip    ☐ Guess: _____    ☐ Look up

**Definition:** _____

## 7 Vocabulary in Context

**Complete each sentence with the correct word from the box.**

| | | | |
|---|---|---|---|
| evolved | implicitly | inherently | insufficiently |
| protocol | rigid | via | virtual |

1. The hospital must get the family's consent to practice lifesaving techniques on the body _____ a form. To get it by verbal means is not allowed.

2. Doctors like to practice on the newly dead because bodies soon become too _____ and aren't flexible enough to work with.

3. Your behavior is _____ disrespectful. It's essentially impolite, and we will not tolerate it.

4. At this hospital, some procedures for getting family consent have _____, but we're not satisfied with them and feel that the procedures still need more work.

5. We're not happy with our current set of rules regarding practicing on recently deceased patients, so we are studying the _____ designed by another hospital.

6. I like the idea of working on _____ cadavers because using a simulation is just as effective as using a real cadaver.

7. So far, alternatives to practicing lifesaving techniques on newly deceased patients have been _____ researched. However, if we work harder on this, I'm sure we'll find better ways to train medical students.

8. They didn't directly state their objections, but by remaining silent, the family _____ gave permission to use their grandfather's body for training purposes.

## 8 Arguments

Follow the directions in the graphic organizer to map the arguments in "Medical Ethics: A Ghastly Way to Practice."

| 1. State the main argument about using recently deceased patients for medical professionals to practice on: |
| --- |
| _____ |
| _____ |
| _____ |

↓

| 2. Present pro arguments (arguments in favor of the practice): |
| --- |
| _____ |
| _____ |
| _____ |

↓

| 3. Present con arguments (arguments against the practice): |
| --- |
| _____ |
| _____ |
| _____ |

↓

| 4. State the author's conclusion: |
| --- |
| _____ |
| _____ |
| _____ |

## 9 Writing a Summary

Use the information from the mapping activity above to write a summary of "Medical Ethics: A Ghastly Way to Practice."

# Writing Focus

## Writing Argumentative Essays

The purpose of an **argumentative essay** is to persuade the reader. You organize an argument essay according to your audience, purpose, thesis, and techniques of support. Here are two ways to organize an argument essay:

**Plan A**

Paragraph 1: introduction and thesis statement

Paragraph 2: 1st pro argument (weakest argument that supports your opinion)

Paragraph 3: pro argument (stronger)

Paragraph 4: pro argument (strongest)

Paragraph 5: con argument and your refutation

Paragraph 6: conclusion and recommendation

**Plan B**

Paragraph 1: introduction and thesis statement

Paragraph 2: con argument and your refutation

Paragraph 3: pro (weakest)

Paragraph 4: pro (stronger)

Paragraph 5: pro (strongest)

Paragraph 6: conclusion

These two plans may have more than one paragraph devoted to pro or con points.

## 1   Analyzing the Structure of an Argument

Look back at the passages in this chapter to review the structure of an argumentative piece of writing on a controversial topic. How is the argument presented in each passage? Does it follow Plan A or Plan B? Or does it have a different structure?

## 2 Writing Assignment

**Choose one of the topics below for your essay for this chapter.**

1. Doctors have the right and the power to attach a do not resuscitate (DNR) order to a patient's chart. They need not consult the family first if they do not think it is necessary—although often they do so.

   Write an argumentative essay in which you present your opinion on what is the right thing to do and try to persuade the reader that you are correct.

2. Animal rights groups are opposed to using animals for scientific purposes in laboratories. Their opponents believe we need to use animals for testing so that human beings can benefit from the scientific breakthroughs.

   Write an argumentative essay in which you present your view in a persuasive manner.

3. When the Olympic Games were held in Seoul, South Korea, the Canadian runner Ben Johnson lost his gold medal because he tested positive for using drugs that were banned. Many Canadians were shocked and disappointed. They argued that athletes from other countries had also used drugs but had not been caught.

   Write an essay in which you try to persuade the reader to accept your point of view regarding the punishment that should be imposed on athletes who are caught using banned drugs.

4. Choose another ethical controversy and write an essay arguing for or against a specific position on the issue.

## 3  Preparing to Write

**The following suggestions may help you plan and organize your paper.**

1.  Take a position on the issue you will be writing about and then write down all the ideas you can. List the arguments on *both* sides—this will help you to better develop the arguments for your side.

2.  Look at the arguments on your side and write your thesis statement, basing it on the information you have gathered so far.

3.  Organize your arguments in order of importance. To have the strongest impact, consider arranging your arguments from least important to most important.

4.  Gather information that supports each of your points. Use facts, examples, personal observation and experiences, quotations, and imagery and cite authorities.

5.  Select methods of development such as comparison, process, and cause/effect that will help you present your opinion in the strongest possible way.

6.  Don't forget to present the other side of the issue—the counterargument. You have seen this in the passages in this chapter. Presenting the counterargument shows the reader that you are well informed and understand the issue as a whole. Use transitions such as the following to introduce the other side of the issue:

    *Some may argue that ...*

    *Critics of this position point out that ...*

    *At this point, contrary opinions must be considered.*

7.  After that, you need to argue against the counterargument, showing that the point may be valid but that it is not strong or important. You must show that the opposing point of view is untrue or incorrect. You need to do this because your reader may believe it rather than accept your opinion or main argument.

## 4  After You Write

**Answer the following questions about your essay. Then revise it.**

1. Is it clear who your audience is?

2. Does your thesis statement express the main idea of your essay?

3. Have you supported the thesis statement with facts, examples, personal observation, and other information?

4. Have you included both pro and con arguments?

5. Do your pro arguments provide strong evidence?

6. Have you refuted the con argument?

7. Does your essay have a logical conclusion?

8. Are your paragraphs connected with appropriate connectors?

## Chapter 7

# Generations

## Chapter Objectives

|  |  |
|---|---|
| **Reading:** | Identifying Mixed Organizational Patterns |
| **Critical Analysis:** | Recognizing Stereotypes |
| **Vocabulary:** | Understanding Idioms in Context |
| **Writing:** | Writing a Critique |

# Reading 1

### 1  Previewing

Preview the reading on page 148. Look at the title. Then read the introduction and the last paragraph.

### 2  Thinking about the Topic

In small groups, discuss your answers to the following questions.

1. Examine the graphs below. What observations can you make about the population of the United States? What observations can you make about the population of Canada?

## Population Graph for the United States

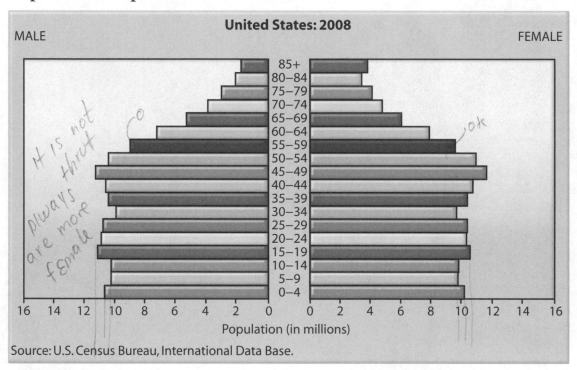

Source: U.S. Census Bureau, International Data Base.

## Population Graph for Canada

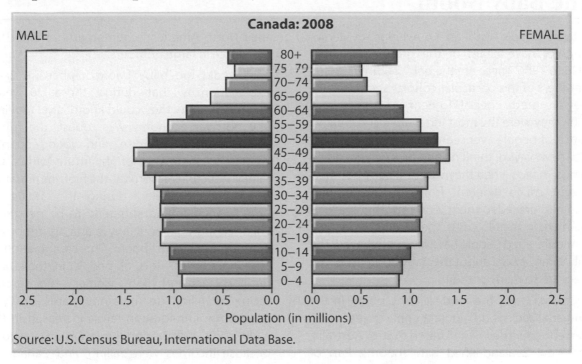

**Canada: 2008**

MALE · FEMALE

Population (in millions)

Source: U.S. Census Bureau, International Data Base.

2. The graphs indicate a bulge in the population of 40- to 60-year-olds in the United States and Canada. Is there a similar bulge in the population of other countries that you are familiar with?

3. What labels do different generations have in the United States? Have different generations been labeled in other countries that you are familiar with? If so, how have they been labeled and why?

## 3 Making Predictions

**In small groups, discuss your answers to the following questions.**

1. What does the expression *baby boom* mean?

2. What might the main idea of "The Baby Boom" be?

3. What details or examples might the author include to develop the main idea?

*Now read the text and answer the questions that follow.*

# The Baby Boom

Even people with no knowledge of demographics have heard of the group born from 1946 to 1966. These are the baby boomers. Some members of this particular cohort* seem to think
5 they are pretty special. To hear them talk, you'd think they were the most innovative and creative bunch of people ever seen, infusing all of society with new ways of thinking and new ways of doing things. In fact, when they were 20, baby boomers
10 weren't much different from the 20-year-olds who had preceded them. And now that many of them are in their late 50s, they are behaving just as middle-aged people have always behaved. The only thing special about the baby boomers is that
15 there are so many of them.

Canada's was the loudest baby boom in the industrialized world. In fact, only three other Western countries—the United States, Australia, and New Zealand—had baby booms. Part of
20 the reason was that these four countries were immigrant receivers, and immigrants tend to be in their 20s, the prime childbearing years. The U.S. boom started earlier, in 1946, and it also ended earlier, in 1964. That's why American periodicals
25 in 1996 were full of articles about baby boomers turning 50, an event that was delayed until 1997 in Canada.

At its peak in 1957, the U.S. boom hit 3.7 children per family, nearly half a baby fewer than
30 Canadian women were producing at the peak of the Canadian boom. The Americans started their boom earlier because more of their war effort was in the Pacific, and the Pacific war wound down sooner. The U.S. troops were brought home
35 in 1945, and kids started appearing in 1946. Canadian troops came home later, so Canadian births did not leap upward until 1947. As for the Australians, they never got much higher than three babies per woman, but they compensated
40 by continuing their boom ten years longer than Canada did. That happened because Australians were slower to adopt the birth control pill and because Australian women were slower than their North American counterparts to enter the
45 workforce in large numbers.

Why did the baby boom happen? A likely explanation is that during those 20 years, Canadians knew they could afford large families. The postwar economy was robust, the future
50 seemed full of promise, and young couples wanted to share that bright future with a big family. A second reason was the high immigration levels that prevailed during the 1950s; as noted earlier, immigrants tend to be people of
55 childbearing age, and they made an important contribution to the boom. The combination of two ingredients—lots of people in their high fertility years and high incomes—is a surefire recipe for filling up maternity wards. But you
60 need both: immigration levels increased in the early 1990s, but the fertility rate didn't respond because incomes were falling, and Canadians, immigrants and nonimmigrants alike, didn't think they could afford extra mouths to feed.

65 Why did the boom end? Toward the end of the 1960s, an increasing number of women were pursuing higher education or entering the workforce. As a result, they were postponing childbirth and deciding to have fewer children.
70 The introduction of the birth control pill made this easier than ever to achieve. The more rapid acceptance of the pill in the United States may explain why the American boom ended before Canada's.

---

*cohort: in a demographic study, a group of individuals who have some statistical factor, such as age, in common

## 4 Comprehension Check

**Write your answers to the following questions.**

1. Who are the baby boomers?

   ..................................................................................................................................

2. What attitude do the authors express toward boomers in paragraph 1? Explain your answer.

   ..................................................................................................................................

   ..................................................................................................................................

3. In the writers' opinion, what makes baby boomers unique?

   ..................................................................................................................................

4. What do the writers mean when they say, "Canada's was the loudest baby boom in the industrialized world"?

   ..................................................................................................................................

5. About how many babies were Canadian women having at the peak of the Canadian boom? How do you know?

   ..................................................................................................................................

   ..................................................................................................................................

6. What do the authors say were the causes of the baby boom?

   ..................................................................................................................................

   ..................................................................................................................................

   ..................................................................................................................................

7. What reasons do the authors give for the end of the baby boom?

   ..................................................................................................................................

   ..................................................................................................................................

## 5 Critical Analysis

**In small groups, discuss your answers to the following questions.**

In what ways can a baby boom affect a society? Think about things such as the economy, the educational system, and cultural trends.

## 6 Vocabulary in Context

**The following sentences are from the reading. For each underlined word, choose the closest meaning: *a, b,* or *c*. You may have to reread the paragraph in order to choose the best meaning.**

1. To hear them talk, you'd think they were the most <u>innovative</u> and creative bunch of people ever seen, infusing all of society with new ways of thinking and new ways of doing things. (para. 1)

   **a.** able to maintain that which is familiar
   **b.** able to think of new ideas
   **c.** able to reproduce

2. In fact, when they were 20, baby boomers weren't much different from the 20-year-olds who had <u>preceded</u> them. (para. 1)

   **a.** come after
   **b.** come at the same time
   **c.** come before

3. Part of the reason was that these four countries were immigrant receivers, and immigrants tend to be in their 20s, the <u>prime</u> childbearing years. (para. 2)

   **a.** best
   **b.** worst
   **c.** safest

4. Canadian troops came home later, <u>so</u> Canadian births did not leap upward until 1947. (para. 3)

   **a.** as a result
   **b.** in addition
   **c.** however

5. As for the Australians, they never got much higher than three babies per woman, but they <u>compensated</u> by continuing their boom ten years longer than Canada did. (para. 3)

   **a.** participated
   **b.** competed
   **c.** balanced this

6. A second reason was the high immigration levels that prevailed during the 1950s; as noted earlier, immigrants tend to be people of childbearing age, and they made an important <u>contribution</u> to the boom. (para. 4)

   **a.** gave a gift
   **b.** participated in
   **c.** had a negative effect on

7. But you need both: immigration levels increased in the early 1990s, but the fertility rate didn't <u>respond</u> because incomes were falling, and Canadians, immigrants and nonimmigrants alike, didn't think they could afford extra mouths to feed. (para. 4)

   **a.** react
   **b.** answer
   **c.** change

**8.** But you need both: immigration levels increased in the early 1990s, but the fertility rate didn't respond because <u>incomes</u> were falling, and Canadians, immigrants and nonimmigrants alike, didn't think they could afford extra mouths to feed. (para. 4)

    **a.** lifestyles

    **b.** money that people earn for working

    **c.** population patterns

---

### Reading ⟼ *Identifying Mixed Organizational Patterns*

In previous chapters, you read about and analyzed a variety of organizational patterns in written texts. Recognizing these patterns while you read helps you remember information and ideas. This is because once you have identified an organizational pattern, you can use that pattern to organize information in your memory.

You've seen patterns for describing objects and processes, comparing and contrasting, showing causes and effects, and persuading. Often, however, you will find that these patterns are combined. For example, an author may use a comparison while showing a cause-and-effect relationship. But even when these patterns are combined, identifying them is still useful as a memory aid.

---

## 7   Identifying Organizational Patterns

Identify the organizational pattern of each of the following paragraphs from "The Baby Boom." Then either outline or draw a map of each paragraph.

Paragraph 1 organizational pattern: ...................................................................

..............................................................................................................................

..............................................................................................................................

..............................................................................................................................

Outline or map: .....................................................................................................

Paragraphs 2 and 3 organizational pattern: ......................................................

..............................................................................................................................

..............................................................................................................................

..............................................................................................................................

Outline or map: .....................................................................................................

Paragraph 4 organizational pattern: ...................................................................

..............................................................................................................................

..............................................................................................................................

..............................................................................................................................

Outline or map: .....................................................................................................

## 8 Working with Organizational Patterns

Rewrite one of the paragraphs in "The Baby Boom" using a different organizational pattern.

# Reading 2

## 1 Previewing

Preview the two readings on pages 153 to 154 and 155 to 157. Look at the titles. Read the introductory paragraph and the last paragraph of each passage. Scan the bulleted list in the first reading.

## 2 Thinking about the Topic

In small groups, discuss your answers to the following questions.

1. Think of all the people you know who were born between the 1970s and the 1990s. Describe them. What characteristics, if any, do they have in common?

2. What is your opinion of characterizing people according to their age group?

## 3 Making Predictions

In small groups, discuss your answers to the following questions.

1. What do you think *Generation Me* means?

2. What do you think is the main idea of the first reading?

3. What details or examples might the author include to develop the main idea?

4. What do you think is the main idea of the second reading?

5. What details or examples might the author include to develop the main idea?

*Now read the text and answer the questions that follow.*

# Generation Me

*The following is an excerpt from the book* Generation Me: Why Today's Young Americans Are More Confident, Assertive, Entitled—and More Miserable—Than Ever Before, *by Jean M. Twenge.*

5 *It's about people born between the 1970s and the 1990s, a group that she calls "GenMe." Twenge used data from 1.3 million young people to show how they differ from previous generations in regard to issues such as self-esteem, individualism, anxiety,*
10 *and sexuality. Born in 1971, Twenge considers herself a member of this generation.*

GenMe's focus on the needs of the individual is not necessarily self-absorbed or isolationist: instead, it's a way of moving through the world
15 beholden to few social rules and with the unshakable belief that you're important. It's also not the same as being spoiled, which implies that we always get what we want; though this probably does describe some kids, it's not the
20 essence of the trend (as I argue in Chapter 4, GenMe's expectations are so great and our reality so challenging that we will probably get less of what we want than any previous generation). We simply take it for granted that we should all
25 feel good about ourselves, we are all special, and we all deserve to follow our dreams. GenMe is straightforward and unapologetic about our self-focus. In 2004's [book] *Conquering Your Quarterlife Crisis*, Jason, 25, relates how he went through
30 some tough times and decided he needed to change things in his life. His new motto was "Do what's best for Jason. I had to make me happy; I had to do what was best for myself in every situation."

35 Our practical orientation toward the self sometimes leaves us with a distaste for boomer abstraction. When a character in the 2004 novel *Something Borrowed* watched the 1980s show *thirtysomething* [about adult baby boomers] as
40 a teen, she wished the boomer characters would "[s]top pondering the meaning of life and start making grocery lists." The matter-of-fact attitude of GenMe appears in everyday language as well—

a language that still includes the abstract concept
45 of self, but uses it in a very simple way, perhaps because we learned the language as children. We speak the language of the self as our native tongue. So much of the common-sense advice that's given these days includes some variation
50 on *self*:

- Worried about how to act in a social situation? "Just be yourself."
- What's the good thing about your alcoholism/drug addiction/
55   murder conviction? "I learned a lot about myself."
- Concerned about your performance? "Believe in yourself." (Often followed by "and anything is possible.")
60 - Should you buy the new pair of shoes or get the nose ring? "Yes, express yourself."
- Why should you leave the unfulfilling relationship/quit the boring
65   job/tell off your mother-in-law? "You have to respect yourself."
- Trying to get rid of a bad habit? "Be honest with yourself."
- Confused about the best time
70   to date or get married? "You have to love yourself before you can love someone else."
- Should you express your opinion? "Yes, stand up for yourself."

75 Americans use these phrases so often that we don't even notice them anymore. [TV psychologist] Dr. Phil, the ultimate in plain-spoken, no-nonsense advice, uttered both "respect yourself" and "stop lying to yourself"
80 within seconds of each other on a *Today* show segment on New Year's resolutions. One of his bestselling books is entitled *Self Matters*. We take these phrases and ideas so much for granted, it's as if we learned them in our sleep as children,

85 like the perfectly conditioned citizens in Aldous Huxley's *Brave New World*.

These aphorisms don't seem absurd to us even when, sometimes, they are. We talk about self-improvement, as if the self could be given better
90 drywall or a new coat of paint. We read self-help books, as if the self could receive tax-deductible donations. The self even has its own magazine (*Self*). Psychologist Martin Seligman says that the traditional self—responsible, hardworking,
95 stern—has been replaced with the "California self," "a self that chooses, feels pleasure and pain, dictates action and even has things like esteem, efficacy, and confidence." Media outlets promote the self relentlessly; I was amazed at how often
100 I heard the word *self* used in the popular media once I started looking for it. A careful study of news stories published or aired between 1980 and 1999 found a large increase in self-reference words (*I, me, mine,* and *myself*) and a marked
105 decrease in collective words (*humanity, country,* or *crowd*).

Young people have learned these self-lessons very well. In a letter to her fans in 2004, Britney Spears, 23, listed her priorities as "'myself, my
110 husband, Kevin, and starting a family." If you had to read that twice to get my point, it's because we take it for granted that we should put ourselves first on our list of priorities—it would be blasphemy if you didn't (unless, of course,
115 you have low self-esteem). Twenty-year-old Maria says her mother often reminds her to consider what other people will think. "It doesn't matter what other people think," Maria insists. "What really matters is how I perceive myself. The real
120 person I need to please is myself."

Smart marketers have figured this out, too. In the late 1990s, [life insurance company] Prudential replaced its longtime insurance slogan "Get a Piece of the Rock" with the nakedly individualistic
125 "Be Your Own Rock." The United States Army, perhaps the last organization one might expect to focus on the individual instead of the group, has followed suit. Its standard slogan, adopted in 2001, is "An Army of One."

## 4  Comprehension Check

**Write your answers to the following questions.**

1. Explain in your own words Twenge's characterization of GenMe. (para. 1)

   ........................................................................................................................................................

   ........................................................................................................................................................

2. According to Twenge, how are members of Generation Me different from boomers? (para. 2)

   ........................................................................................................................................................

3. How do the examples in Twenge's bulleted list support her argument?

   ........................................................................................................................................................

   ........................................................................................................................................................

4. What difference in how people define themselves did Twenge notice between 1980 and 1999? (para. 4)

   ........................................................................................................................................................

5. Explain Twenge's Britney Spears quote. How does it support her argument? (para. 5)

   ........................................................................................................................................................

   ........................................................................................................................................................

*Now read the text and answer the questions that follow.*

# Book Review: *Generation Me: Why Today's Young Americans Are More Confident, Assertive, Entitled— and More Miserable—Than Ever Before*
## By Jean M. Twenge, Ph.D. (Free Press, 2006)

Review by Aaron Shulman

As a 23-year-old American who considers himself mildly confident and assertive but neither miserable nor entitled, I was curious to see what Jean M. Twenge, a San Diego State Univer-
5 sity psychology professor in her mid-30s, had to say in her new book, *Generation Me: Why Today's Young Americans Are More Confident, Assertive, Entitled—and More Miserable—Than Ever Before.*

Twenge saddles herself with the task of
10 describing the defining characteristics of the children of baby boomers born from 1970 to the end of the twentieth century, a group she terms "Generation Me." The members of this generation, while remarkably diverse in many respects,
15 share a unifying aspect: we are "unapologetically focused on the individual," a trait inherited from our boomer parents and fanned to extremes by the culture they engendered.

While no one—especially a generation raised
20 to worship individualism—likes to have their sameness within a group pointed out to them, I was struck by how consistently Twenge's general-

izations about GenMe rang true about me and most of my friends. We think of work more as a path toward self-fulfillment than as a means to a stable livelihood; we feel we can have it all and believe in "following our dreams" and doing things our own way; we heed social rules and figures of authority only insofar as they don't get in our way; and we view our 20s as a period to bounce around and "find ourselves," because otherwise we won't be ready for married family life in our late 20s and early 30s. As to whether these trends are good or bad, Twenge only occasionally makes an outright judgment, letting her research instead speak for itself. And most of the time her research convincingly shows—though it never hurts to be reminded that her data and sources are selectively mediated by her—that these developments have no small hand in creating the doldrums of the book's subtitle.

In sketching out how these conditions came to be, Twenge tells an engaging story, fueled and supported by a solid base of data, illustrative quotes from her and others' research, and barometric examples from TV shows, movies, comics, and advertisements. She explains how the defiance of authority and shirking of social approval pioneered by boomers in the '60s and '70s was subsumed by the mainstream and incorporated into the status quo, informing GenMe's view of the world. Twenge also serves up a well-argued critique of the self-esteem industry in the United States, which she says has a narcissistic-tinged ethos that is harming America's youth vastly more than it helps. Throughout the book, her analyses of myriad topics articulated a number of ideas on the tip of my mind's tongue, getting me to think about myself and my parents, as well the culture we come from and help create.

*Generation Me* is cogent, thoughtful, and fun to read, but over the course of the book, I couldn't shake my discomfort with the sensationalistic use of the word *miserable* to describe my generation. In spite of all the dispiriting trends that dog GenMe—depression, crushing disappointment when the real world doesn't deliver on the things we've been taught to expect, credit card debt, mountainous student loans, divorce-like breakups, rising health insurance premiums and real estate prices, estrangement from the community—to say we're miserable seems to preclude resilience. Yes, GenMe must confront some bleak obstacles, but doesn't every generation? Thinking of ourselves as miserable doesn't seem to be a move in the right direction. Twenge does realize this, in a sense, and closes her book with prescriptive optimism: "Generation Me needs realistic expectations, careful career guidance, and assistance when we become parents. In return, we will gladly lend our energy and ambition toward our work and toward helping others."

## 5   Analyzing a Model

**Referring to the book review, write your answers to the following questions.**

**A. Questions for Analysis: Content**

  **1.** What was Twenge's purpose for writing *Generation Me*?

  ......................................................................................................................................

  **2.** What do you learn about the book from reading this review?

  ......................................................................................................................................

3. In the opinion of the reviewer, how successfully does the author of *Generation Me* achieve her purpose?

.................................................................................................................

.................................................................................................................

**B. Questions for Analysis: Structure**

1. Where does the name of the book first appear?

.................................................................................................................

2. Where is the purpose of the book discussed?

.................................................................................................................

3. Why might the reviewer describe himself at the beginning of the review?

.................................................................................................................

4. Which paragraphs discuss the strengths of the book? Where does the reviewer discuss the limitations of the book?

.................................................................................................................

5. What explanations or examples does the reviewer give to clarify his points?

.................................................................................................................

.................................................................................................................

.................................................................................................................

6. To what extent does the writer of the review use direct quotations from the original text?

.................................................................................................................

.................................................................................................................

7. How frequently does the author of the review refer to the book by name?

.................................................................................................................

8. Are there any points in the critique that are unclear? How might the writer of the review clarify these points?

.................................................................................................................

.................................................................................................................

.................................................................................................................

9. How does the writer conclude his review?

.................................................................................................................

.................................................................................................................

10. As a reader of the critique, are you satisfied with the conclusion? Why or why not?

.................................................................................................................

.................................................................................................................

## 6 Critical Analysis

**In small groups, discuss your answers to the following questions.**

1. In your opinion, does Twenge's assessment of people born between the 1970s and the 1990s apply only to Americans? Explain your answer.

2. Do you agree with Twenge's assessment of people born between the 1970s and the 1990s? Why or why not?

### Vocabulary ➟ *Understanding Idioms in Context*

**Idioms** are phrases that have a special meaning. However, the meaning usually has little to do with the literal meaning of the individual words in the phrases. This sometimes makes idioms difficult to understand. However, when you are reading, you can often use the context of idioms to guess their meaning.

For example, in paragraph 2 of the book review, the author says, "Twenge <u>saddles herself with</u> the task of describing the defining characteristics of the children of baby boomers." To *saddle oneself with* something is an idiom. The meaning doesn't have anything to do with the word *saddle*, something you sit on when you ride a horse. Rather, to *saddle oneself with* something means to take on a responsibility. You can guess this from the context, especially because the phrase is followed by the word *task*.

## 7 Understanding Idioms in Context

**Find and read the following idioms in context in "Generation Me" (1) and the book review (2). Then match them with their meanings. Discuss your answers with a partner.**

| | |
|---|---|
| .......... 1. tell off (1: bulleted list) | a. deliver |
| .......... 2. stand up for (1: bulleted list) | b. sound true |
| .......... 3. take for granted (1: para. 1) | c. almost able to be remembered |
| .......... 4. follow suit (1: para. 6) | d. go from place to place |
| .......... 5. ring true (2: para. 3) | e. show little attention to |
| .......... 6. bounce around (2: para. 3) | f. be part of |
| .......... 7. find oneself (2: para. 3) | g. speak angrily to |
| .......... 8. have a hand in (2: para. 3) | h. learn about oneself |
| .......... 9. serve up (2: para. 4) | i. defend |
| .......... 10. at the tip of one's tongue (2: para. 4) | j. do the same thing |

## 8 Vocabulary in Context

**Guess the meanings of the underlined words in sentences from "Generation Me" (1) and the book review (2). Write your guesses on the lines. You may have to reread the paragraph in order to guess the meaning.**

1. Our practical <u>orientation</u> toward the self sometimes leaves us with a distaste for boomer abstraction. (1)

   ...........................................................................................................................................

2. The matter-of-fact attitude of GenMe appears in everyday language as well—a language that still includes the <u>abstract</u> concept of self, but uses it in a very simple way, perhaps because we learned the language as children. (1)

   ...........................................................................................................................................

3. GenMe is <u>straightforward</u> and unapologetic about our self-focus. (1)

   ...........................................................................................................................................

4. Young people have learned these self-lessons very well. In a letter to her fans in 2004, Britney Spears, 23, listed her <u>priorities</u> as "myself, my husband, Kevin, and starting a family." (1)

   ...........................................................................................................................................

5. The members of this generation, while remarkably <u>diverse</u> in many respects, share a <u>unifying</u> aspect: we are "unapologetically focused on the individual," a trait inherited from our boomer parents and fanned to extremes by the culture they engendered. (2)

   diverse: ...............................................................................................................................

   unifying: .............................................................................................................................

6. We heed social rules and figures of <u>authority</u> only insofar as they don't get in our way; and we view our 20s as a period to bounce around and "find ourselves," because otherwise we won't be ready for married family life in our late 20s and early 30s. (2)

   ...........................................................................................................................................

7. And most of the time her research convincingly shows—though it never hurts to be reminded that her data and sources are selectively <u>mediated</u> by her—that these developments have no small hand in creating the doldrums of the book's subtitle. (2)

   ...........................................................................................................................................

## 9 Responding to a Text

**Write your own response to Twenge's ideas, based on the excerpt you read of *Generation Me*.**

# Reading 3

## 1  Previewing

Preview the reading on pages 161 to 162. Read the title. Then read the first paragraph and the last paragraph.

## 2  Thinking about the Topic

In small groups, discuss your answers to the following questions.

1. What was happening in your country or in the world when you were young? Think of major political, economic, and cultural events.

2. In what ways did these events affect the way you view the world? In what way did they define your generation?

3. In your opinion, what are the positive characteristics of your generation? What are the negative characteristics?

## 3  Making Predictions

In small groups, discuss your answers to the following questions.

1. What do you think a *global citizen* is?

2. What might be the main idea of this reading?

3. What details or examples might the author include to develop the main idea?

*Now read the text and answer the questions that follow.*

# The New Global Citizens

A funny thing has happened as Generation Y has been growing up. The country made a mid-course change, and that led to a generational change. The youngest generation was first described in the mid-'90s as the Millennial Generation because it would span the period from 1980 to 2002, bridging the new millennium. But a generation is defined not so much by *when* its members were born as when they were *young*. Each generation forms core values that remain with its members throughout their lives, based on the events and circumstances that surrounded them during their formative years.

The Millennials were born during a time of economic growth and stability in the United States. The economy changed after the tragedy of September 11, 2001. Defining events, such as the assassinations of John F. Kennedy and Martin Luther King, Jr.; the Watergate scandal; Neil Armstrong on the moon; the *Challenger* explosion; the Oklahoma City bombing; and September 11 have profound and lasting effects on the generational psyche. Combine a major event with dramatic shifts in the economy and national security, and younger children begin to have a different life experience from those just ahead of them.

Such a shift happened for the Millennials, also known as Generation Y. The country changed, the economy changed, the pace of change itself quickened, and now demographers are calling this cohort that covers the span from 1978 to 1994 "Global Citizens."

When talking of generational characteristics, there is always a danger of being accused of stereotyping. In this short article, I will do a broad sweep of this generation, and I will make generalizations that can be challenged by many exceptions to the rule. I recognize that we are products of many influences, such as urban or rural lifestyle, birth order, and gender. However, unique forces, such as the growth and demise of the dot.com bubble, incidences of school violence, overly involved parents, and the rapid pace of change in the world, have shaped Generation Y. To better understand them, it is helpful to identify specific characteristics that may appear in varying degrees in the members of this generation.

So what makes this civic minded, globally aware, well-educated, and diverse generation different? The following are some characteristics, both positive and negative.

First and foremost, Gen Yers are impatient. Life has always moved at a very fast pace. The old adage "good things come to those who wait" has no meaning for this generation. The Internet has taught them there is no need to wait for anything—everything is available at the click of a button, from test grades to chat rooms. Previous generations were accustomed to going to the library to look up information in the card catalog and then finding the books and searching for the answers. For Generation Y, the concept of going to the library to find information is foreign. It is instantly available through a Google search. There is no need to look up a movie time in the newspaper, when they can access the information with their cell phones. Gen Yers have grown up with computers in the classroom, video games, and MTV. They like to be entertained and stimulated across all their senses. They become restless and bored quickly and are constantly looking for the next level of challenge.

Living in a time of constant change has made this generation very adaptable. They have never had time to become stuck in old patterns or routines. They process information quickly and embrace change. They are progressive, forward thinkers, because they are not wedded to or even interested in history. Life is about what is ahead and how quickly you can react or adapt. Gen Yers question everything because their thinking is not framed in the past. They are open to an endless stream of new possibilities. To avoid boredom, they have become natural innovators, unafraid of new ideas and new approaches. They are not simply comfortable with technology; they are creating new levels of technology.

Gen Yers have lived lives filled with activities and are thus skilled time managers and multi-taskers. They have learned to balance sports, school, jobs, and social time. They strive for maximum results with minimal effort. They are very efficient and do not get caught up in details. They possess a self-confidence that allows them analyze problems, select options, and move on. They do not sit around and wait for things to happen when they know they can make things happen.

This generation has lived in a time when the media and tell-all books debunked all past heroes. They watched the confessions of Princess Diana, saw sports figures discredited, and heard a president lie. They have few illusions about what the world is really like and thus are skeptical and wary. They have seen too much to believe everything at face value. Because their skepticism has led them to question much of what they see and hear, Gen Yers value honesty and truth. They dislike embellishments, half-truths, and overinflated promises.

Exposed to far more, at an earlier age, than previous generations, these young people have seen the good, the bad, and the ugly. Gen Yers are sometimes labeled as street-smart, and in fact, there is very little they have not seen, through the media or virtually. They are resilient, slow to be shocked, quick to react, and willing to take risks. Life has been an adventure of constant change, and they feel well equipped to tackle any situation. If you have established a relationship of honesty and trust, they will stick with you through anything. Many adults label this generation as disrespectful and outspoken. They address their elders as equals, using first names rather than *Mr.* or *Mrs.* While they like older people (especially the veteran generation) and respect their life experiences, they are not awed or overly impressed by anyone or anything. Though they often appear disrespectful, Gen Yers

crave respect. They believe that power equals respect. While they are slow to give respect, they expect respect automatically.

"Children should be seen and not heard" has not been the axiom of this generation. They have been included in family decision making from their earliest days. They have been taught to speak up, and their opinions have been considered and valued. They are very independent thinkers and feel very comfortable sharing their ideas and opinions with anyone. In a recent workshop on this topic, a young member of the audience immediately spoke up when I stated this generation tends to be bluntly outspoken. She related that her coworkers often criticize her for being blunt, when she believes she is being honest and open and giving immediate feed-back. What her coworkers saw as "attitude" was authenticity to her.

Diversity is a value for members of this generation, and thus they display an incredible tolerance and a slowness to judge other people. Though adults sometimes challenge this, saying Gen Yers can be rude and outspoken, these young people have a great spirit of openness. True products of the civil rights movement, they do not display the same prejudices that divided earlier generations. They are great team members, ignoring gender and racial biases to work with anyone to accomplish common goals.

Finally, Gen Yers are looking for ways to make their mark and find their causes. I have had groups of young people tell me they are looking for their purpose and something to believe in. But they also expect you to believe in them. They want to be respected, and when they find that fit, they will be faithful allies.

In sum, their adaptability, acceptance of new ideas, outspokenness, and tolerance make Gen Ys highly committed and fiercely loyal Global Citizens.

## 4  Comprehension Check

**Write your answers to the following questions.**

1. In paragraph 1, the author states his thesis. What is it?

   ............................................................................................................................

2. What are *defining events*? How do they affect a generation according to the author?

   ............................................................................................................................

   ............................................................................................................................

3. List the characteristics of Generation Y, as expressed in paragraphs 6–13.

   ............................................................................................................................

   ............................................................................................................................

   ............................................................................................................................

   ............................................................................................................................

4. What type of example does the author use in paragraph 11 to support his point?

   ............................................................................................................................

5. Why might the author say that some of the characteristics of Generation Y are positive and some are negative? Give examples from the passage of each type.

   ............................................................................................................................

   ............................................................................................................................

6. From what country or culture are the young people the author is writing about? How can you tell? Do the characteristics of young people from this culture apply to young people in other cultures? Explain your answer.

   ............................................................................................................................

   ............................................................................................................................

   ............................................................................................................................

7. Do you agree that members of Generation Y are global citizens? Why or why not?

   ............................................................................................................................

   ............................................................................................................................

## 5   Recognizing Stereotypes

**In small groups, discuss your answers to the following questions.**

1. What are some of the stereotypes expressed in the passages in this chapter about baby boomers and members of Generation Me (also called Generation Yers)? What are some other generational stereotypes that you are aware of?

2. In paragraph 4 of "The New Global Citizens," the author refers to his own use of stereotypes. Why might he have done this?

## 6   Understanding Idioms in Context

**Find the following idioms in context in "The New Global Citizens." Guess their meanings from their contexts and write your guesses on the lines.**

1. at face value (para. 9): ................................................................................................

2. the good, the bad, and the ugly (para. 10): ........................................................

3. street-smart (para. 10): .............................................................................................

## 7  Vocabulary in Context

For each of the underlined words in the following sentences from "The New Global Citizens," choose the best definition from the list below. Write the number of the sentence next to the definition.

1. I will do a broad sweep of this generation, and I will make generalizations that can be <u>challenged</u> by many exceptions to the rule. (para. 4)

2. However, <u>unique</u> forces, such as the growth and demise of the dot.com bubble, the Columbine High School shootings, overly involved parents, and the rapid pace of change in the world, have shaped Generation Y. (para. 4)

3. To better understand them, it is helpful to identify specific characteristics that may appear in <u>varying</u> degrees in the members of this generation. (para. 4)

4. Living in a time of <u>constant</u> change has made this generation very adaptable. (para. 7)

5. To avoid boredom, they have become natural innovators, unafraid of new ideas and new <u>approaches</u>. (para. 7)

6. They strive for maximum results with <u>minimal</u> effort. (para. 8)

7. <u>Exposed</u> to far more, at an earlier age, than previous generations, these young people have seen the good, the bad, and the ugly. (para. 10)

8. <u>Diversity</u> is a value for members of this generation, and thus they display an incredible tolerance and a slowness to judge other people. (para. 12)

### Definitions

.................. **a.** the smallest amount

.................. **b.** exceptional; the only one of its kind

.................. **c.** different

.................. **d.** ways of doing things

.................. **e.** continual; not stopping

.................. **f.** shown; having seen

.................. **g.** disputed; argued against

.................. **h.** the condition or quality of being different

## 8  Writing a Summary

Write a one-paragraph summary of "The New Global Citizens."

# Writing Focus

## Critiques

You analyzed the organization of the review of "Generation Me" on page 157. You can organize a review in several ways. The following diagrams show two possibilities.

**Organizational Pattern 1**

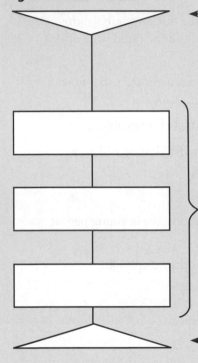

← **Introduction**
- Name of author, title of article
- Short summary of major points to be analyzed
- Your thesis; opinion about the main points of the article

**Body**

Each body paragraph can contain the following:
- The major point to be analyzed in that paragraph
- Direct quotes from the article demonstrating the point being made (optional)
- Your topic sentence, which states agreement or disagreement with the main point
- Your proof of the effectiveness or ineffectiveness of that major point: facts, examples, physical descriptions, and/or personal experiences
- Perhaps a suggestion for improving the author's major point

← **Conclusion**
- Perhaps only one sentence
- Probably an opinion that you have proved within your critique

**Organizational Pattern 2**

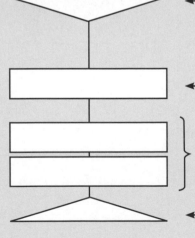

← **Introduction**
- Name of author, title of article
- Short summary of major points to be analyzed
- Thesis statement of your opinion

← **Summary paragraph**
- Objective, complete, balanced summary of article

**Body paragraphs of analysis**
- Point to be analyzed
- Topic sentence (agree or disagree)
- Support for your opinion

← **Conclusion**
- Final response to essay
- Prediction, solution, or recommendation

# 1 Analyzing Critique Structure

**With a partner, discuss your answers to the following questions.**

1. Which organizational pattern does the review of *Generation Me* follow?

2. When might one model be more suitable than the other?

## Writing a Critique

### Reading the Original Text

Review the information on writing a summary in Chapter 1, page 24. Remember, your purpose is to discover the author's main purpose or point and to draw out the important supporting points. For a critique, however, you should also make note of your responses to the passage as you read, especially in regard to any strengths or weaknesses that you discover in it.

Your responses to the passage may not be well developed. You may simply have a question about an idea discussed in the text. You may see connections or contradictions with other materials you have read. You may see contradictions within the passage itself.

It is important that you record all of these impressions since you may not remember them later when you are writing your critique. You can record them in note form in the margins of the passage or take notes on a piece of paper. If you take notes, be sure to include page numbers.

### Writing

1. Think about the significance of the author's main idea. Think about how well the author achieved his or her purpose. Depending on the passage that you are reviewing, you might also consider the following questions:

   • What did the author use for sources? Are these sources current?

   • Which school of thought do the ideas in the text belong to? What are the strengths within this perspective? Does the author successfully overcome any of the limitations of this school of thought?

   • Does the text make an important contribution to its field? When it was published, did it introduce new ideas, or was it a restatement of older ideas?

2. Write a preliminary thesis statement that expresses your view of the text.

3. Find support for your thesis statement. Depending on the formality of the assignment, this could come from your own experience or from source texts. What support can you find for your position? To a great extent, the effectiveness of your critique will depend on the quality of the support that you find for your position.

4. List the points you will use to support your thesis statement. Be sure that you are critiquing significant points from the article or book.

5. Plan your critique. Which model will you use? Will you summarize the original text first and then critique the ideas, or will you integrate the summary and the critique?

6. Write a first draft of your critique.

   • Refer to the names of the author and the text often enough to keep your reader's attention.

   • It is sometimes a good idea to include direct quotations from the original source that illustrate the author's points especially well. In most instances, however, you should use your own words to paraphrase and summarize.

## 2  Planning a Critique

Reread "The New Global Citizens." As you read, jot down notes on the author's main purpose and the important supporting points. Then go through Steps 1 to 5 in the box above to plan a critique of "The New Global Citizens."

## 3  Writing Assignment

Choose one of the topics below for your essay for this chapter.

1. Write a critique of approximately 200 to 250 words of "The New Global Citizens."

2. Write a critique of approximately 200 to 250 words of an article or book of your own choice.

   Refer back to "Writing a Critique" on page 167. Remember that the process suggested in this section may not fit this particular writing situation exactly; you may need to modify it to suit your own needs.

## 4  After You Write

Answer the following questions about your essay. Then revise it.

1. Have you named the text and authors and briefly stated the main idea of the original text in your introduction?

2. Does your thesis statement express a clear position?

3. Have you sufficiently summarized the original text in the body of your critique?

4. Is the position in your thesis statement consistently supported in the body of your critique?

5. Have you supplied convincing reasons for your own analysis of the text?

6. Have you used a balance of direct quotations, paraphrases, and summary statements?

## Chapter 8

# Life Online:
## The Impact of Social Networks

Invite | Blog | Browse | Favorites | Events | [                    ] ( Social Networking ) ( Search )

## Sara

Female
17 years old
MyTown, IL
United States

Last Login: Yesterday

### Contacting Sara

- ☐ Send Message
- ☐ Forward to Friend
- ☐ Add to Friends
- ☐ Add to Favorites
- ☐ Instant Message
- ☐ Block User
- ☐ Add to Group
- ☐ Rank User

### Sara's Friends

**Sara has 572 friends.**

| Jen | Scott | Meghan |
|---|---|---|
|  |   | |

| Christina | Lissy | Michelle |
|---|---|---|
|  |  |  |

**Chad wrote**
**at 11:40 am**

Hi, Sara! Hope the History exam went well. Call me tonight! :D

Write on Jessica's Page | Message | Delete

**Jen wrote**
**at 11:20 am**

Did you watch the show last night?

Write on Jen's Page | Message | Delete

**Scott wrote**
**at 9:40 am**

Sorry I missed your brother's birthday.

Write on Scott's Page | Message | Delete

**Lindsey wrote**
**at 11:40 pm**

Hi, Sara. Do you know who is pitching Saturday? I haven't talked to coach yet.

Write on Lindsey's Page | Message | Delete

**Trent wrote**
**at 7:40 pm**

Tomorrow is Friday! Yay!

Write on Nicky's Page | Message | Delete

**Lissy wrote**
**at 7:40 pm**

Hi, Sara! Good luck on the History exam. Let me know how it goes.

Write on Joe's Page | Message | Delete

**Brianna wrote**
**at 7:20 pm**

Anything going on tonight?

Write on Brianna's Page | Message | Delete

## Chapter Objectives

| | |
|---|---|
| **Reading:** | Taking Notes for a Research Paper |
| | Analyzing a Problem-Solution Passage |
| **Critical Analysis:** | Synthesizing Information |
| **Vocabulary:** | Recognizing and Using Lead-in Expressions |
| **Writing:** | Writing a Research Paper |
| | Documenting Sources |

# Reading 1

## 1 Previewing

Preview the two readings on pages 172 to 173 and 174 to 175. Look at the titles. Read the introductory paragraph and the last paragraph of each passage. Scan the bulleted list in the first reading.

## 2 Thinking about the Topic

In small groups, discuss your answers to the following questions.

1. How much do you use the Internet? What do you use it for?

2. What are some of the advantages of the Internet? What are some of the disadvantages?

## 3 Making Predictions

In small groups, discuss your answers to the following questions.

1. What do you think *social networking* means?

2. What do you think is the main idea of "Social Networking Sites and Teens"?

3. What details or examples might the author include to develop the main idea?

4. What do you think is the main idea of "Web of Risks"?

5. What details or examples might the author include to develop the main idea?

## 4 Scanning

**Scan the report below to learn more about the use of social networking sites among teens. Try to answer all the questions within ten minutes.**

1. What percentage of young people who are online use social networking sites?

2. The information in the report is based on a survey. Give the following information about the survey:
   a. Who conducted the survey?
   b. When was the survey conducted?
   c. How many people were surveyed?
   d. What were their ages?
   e. How was the survey conducted?

3. Name two popular social networking sites.

4. What percentage of teens have online profiles that not everyone can see?

5. What percentage of girls ages 15–17 have used an online social network? What percentage of boys the same age have used an online social network?

6. What percentage of teens use social networking sites to make new friends?

7. Who is more likely to use social networking sites to make new friends, boys or girls?

8. Who is more likely to use social networking sites to flirt (show that they are attracted to another person), boys or girls?

*Now read the text and answer the questions that follow.*

# Social Networking Sites and Teens

According to a national survey of teenagers conducted by the Pew Internet & American Life Project, more than half (55 percent) of all online American youths ages 12–17 use online social
5 networking sites. A social networking site is an online place where a user can create a profile and build a personal network that connects him or her to other users.

The survey finds that older teens, particularly
10 girls, are more likely to use these sites. For girls, social networking sites are primarily places to reinforce preexisting friendships; for boys, the networks also provide opportunities for flirting and making new friends.

15 In the past five years, such sites have rocketed from a niche activity into a phenomenon that engages tens of millions of Internet users. The explosive growth in the popularity of these sites has generated concerns among some parents,
20 school officials, and government leaders about the potential risks posed to young people when personal information is made available in such a public setting.

The survey, conducted by telephone from
25 October 23 through November 19, 2006, among a national sample of 935 youths ages 12–17, asked about the ways that teenagers use these sites and their reasons for doing so.

**Among the key findings:**

- Some 55 percent of online teens
30 have created a personal profile online, and 55 percent have used social networking sites like MySpace or Facebook.

- Of teens who have created a profile,
35 66 percent say that their profile is not visible to all Internet users. They limit access to their profiles.

- Some 48 percent of teens visit social networking Web sites daily or more
40 often: 26 percent visit once a day, and 22 percent visit several times a day.

- Older girls ages 15–17 are more likely to have used social networking sites and to have created online profiles:
45 70 percent of older girls have used an online social network compared with 54 percent of older boys, and 70 percent of older girls have created an online profile, while only 57
50 percent of older boys have done so.

Teens say social networking sites help them manage their friendships.

- Some 91 percent of all social networking teens say they use the
55 sites to stay in touch with friends they see frequently, while 82 percent use the sites to stay in touch with friends they rarely see in person.

- Among social networking teens,
60 72 percent use the sites to make plans with friends; 49 percent use the sites to make new friends.

- Older boys who use social networking sites (ages 15–17) are
65 more likely than girls of the same age to say that they use social networking sites to make new friends (60 percent vs. 46 percent).

- Just 17 percent of all social
70 networking teens say they use the sites to flirt.

- Older boys who use social networking sites are more than twice as likely as older girls to
75 say they use the sites to flirt; 29 percent report this compared with just 13 percent of older girls.

**Note**

We define social networking Web sites here as sites where users can create a profile and connect
80 that profile to other profiles for the purposes of making an explicit personal network. However, in the telephone survey from which the data in this

memo were derived, we allowed the respondent to define social networking Web sites, prompting
85 with two examples of such sites—Facebook and MySpace.

### Source Information

Title of Article: "Social Networking Sites and Teens"

Authors: Amanda Lenhart and Mary Madden

Publication: Report, Pew Research Center Publications

Date/Issue: January 7, 2007

URL: http://pewresearch.org/pubs/118/social-networking-websites-and-teens

## Reading ➦ *Taking Notes for a Research Paper*

In this chapter, you are going to read several articles about issues related to online networking sites and then write a research paper. Your paper will discuss the concerns that some people have about social networking sites and present some ways to alleviate these concerns. Therefore, as you read, it will be important to think about this topic and gather information that you can use in your paper.

One way to take notes for a research paper is to use index cards. Keep a set by you as you read and write down information from your reading that you think will be useful later. Use one card for each fact you want to record; don't put two facts on one card. In most cases, you will need to paraphrase this information in your essay, so write the fact in your own words without looking at the original. If you copy any information word for word, however, be sure to put quotation marks around it.

At the top of the card, include complete source information for your fact: the name of the publication, the author(s), the publishing company (for a book or report), the date of the publication, and the page numbers on which you found the information. If the information is from a journal or magazine, include the article title and the name of the journal or magazine, along with the volume and issue number, if those are provided. If the information is from a Web site, also include the URL, the page number or paragraph in which you found the information, and the date and time that you found the information.

> "Social Networking Sites and Teens"
> http://pewresearch.org/pubs/118/social-networking-websites-and-teens
> by Amanda Lenhart and Mary Madden
> Pew Research Center Publications
> January 7, 2007
> para. 8
> April 6, 2009, 4:15 p.m.
> Older teen girls (15–17) are more likely to have used social networking sites than boys—70 percent as opposed to 54 percent.

You will learn more about citing sources later in this chapter.

## 5 Taking Notes for a Research Paper

Now read the next passage. Take notes as you read. Use index cards or pieces of paper for the facts that you want to record for your essay. Note the source information that follows the passage.

# Web of Risks

Cameron Walker learned the hard way that sharing information online can have unintended consequences. In 2005, the sophomore at Fisher College in Boston organized a student petition
5 dedicated to getting a campus police guard fired and posted it on the popular college social network Facebook.com. Walker wrote that the guard "loves to antagonize students ... and needs to be eliminated." It was a poor choice of words.
10 Another student informed school officials, who logged on and interpreted the comments as threatening. Though Walker claimed he was trying only to expose the guard's demeanor, he was expelled. He's now enrolled at another
15 college and admits he made a serious mistake. "I was a naive 21-year-old," he says.

Creating a page on a social networking site is now a cherished form of self-expression at universities around the world. Students use ad-
20 supported services like Facebook, MySpace, TagWorld, and Bebo to make friends, plan their social lives, and project their personalities. The most popular site among college students is Facebook, with more than eight million members.
25 A student's personal Facebook page is usually a revealing, dynamic chronicle of campus life— one clearly not meant for the eyes of parents, teachers, or anyone else older than 25.

But adults are taking notice. Sites like
30 Facebook are accessible to nearly anyone willing to spend the time to gain access: teachers, school administrators, and even potential employers and the police. Such online services can create the illusion of privacy where none actually
35 exists. Facebook, in particular, was designed to emphasize privacy and intimacy. Only other users at your school (with the same college e-mail domain name), and those in networks you

join, can see your home page. But determined
40 off-campus visitors can persuade a student or alumnus to help them access the student's page.

What happens when the identity you reveal to friends suddenly overwhelms the facade you present to grown-ups? The results can be
45 awkward—or worse. Photos from drunken parties, recollections of sexual escapades, profanity, or threats—all these indiscretions, posted online, have gotten students suspended or expelled or have harmed job prospects. In a couple of
50 decades, a presidential candidate may be called on to answer for a college misadventure that he or she impetuously detailed in a blog entry.

Harvard student Marc Zuckerberg and a few classmates designed Facebook in 2003 to facil-
55 itate contact among students. After it was launched in early 2004, the service spread like the flu in a freshman dorm, first at Harvard and then to all 2,100 four-year colleges. Last year the company opened its digital doors to high schoolers.
60 Early on, Zuckerberg left college and moved his fledgling enterprise to Silicon Valley, raising more than $35 million in venture capital. Facebook now has 100 employees and is supported by big advertisers like Apple and MasterCard.

65 Facebook's founders worried about privacy. That's why it isn't one big network but a series of connected smaller ones. "We decided early on that you get better information flow and more trust if you limit access to just those around
70 you," says Zuckerberg. Besides restricting access to a student's classmates, Facebook offers extra privacy tools. Students can limit parts of their pages, such as photos, to specific people. Still, just 17 percent of customers ever change those
75 privacy settings.

For many students, Facebook is not only an interactive diary and yearbook but also a pervasive way to stay in touch. Mitchell Perley, an Atlanta-born student at the University of Edinburgh in Scotland, is typical. His page includes a photo with a friend at Disneyland, mentions of his membership in such Facebook groups as the Krispy Kreme [doughnut] Appreciation Society, and listings of his favorite musicians and films. Perhaps most important, his page is linked to the pages of 99 friends at his college and 845 back home at various U.S. schools.

But not everyone's Facebook experiences have been positive. Brad Davis was a freshman at Emory University in Atlanta in 2005 when he and friends commemorated a night of drinking by posting photos of themselves in their dorm, hoisting their libations. They created a Facebook group called the Dobbs 2nd Floor Alcoholics, named after their dorm. A dorm adviser saw the photos and reported the underage imbibers. The school ordered Davis and his friends to hang anti-drinking posters on their walls, and a citation went on their records.

Students' indiscriminate postings may also get them into trouble when they're applying for a job or to graduate school. The postings could still be accessible online despite students' efforts to delete them. Even though companies are loath to admit it, researching candidates on social networks is becoming as easy and prevalent as entering their names into Google. Laurie Sybel, a director of career development at Vermont Technical College, had never looked at Facebook until she got a call from a big company about the internship application of a 19-year-old. The student was being rejected, Sybel recalls, because executives had viewed the student's Facebook page, which contained a photo of him holding a bottle of vodka. The company noted that the student not only was apparently breaking the law but also was demonstrating bad judgment by publishing the photo. In response, Vermont Technical, like other colleges, now integrates tips for social network decorum into its career guidance workshops.

Not all students want to temper their behavior. They point out that the Internet lets them express themselves and find like-minded souls. Still, adults aren't likely to stop prying anytime soon. That means students who use Facebook and MySpace have a new burden. The Web may seem ephemeral, but what you casually post one night might just last a digital eternity. While social networking represents a powerful tool for today's students, they're advised to be prudent—even if they have no plans to run for president someday.

**Source Information**

Title of Article: "Web of Risks"

Author: Brad Stone

Publication: *Newsweek* magazine

Date/Issue: August 21, 2006

Page: 76

## 6  Comparing Notes

**Compare your notes with a partner and answer the following questions.**

As you read "Web of Risks," what information seemed useful? What did you take notes on? Did you miss anything that your partner noticed? Revise your notes, if necessary.

## 7 Comprehension Check

**Write your answers to the following questions. Try to use your notes.**

1. What is the main idea of "Web of Risks"?

   ................................................................................................................

   ................................................................................................................

2. What does the author mean when he says, "Such online services can create the illusion of privacy where none actually exists"? (para. 3)

   ................................................................................................................

   ................................................................................................................

3. How has Facebook tried to deal with the issue of privacy? Has this worked? Why or why not?

   ................................................................................................................

   ................................................................................................................

4. What is an example of a positive experience that college students can have with social networking sites?

   ................................................................................................................

   ................................................................................................................

   ................................................................................................................

5. What are some of the negative experiences that college students have had with social networking sites?

   ................................................................................................................

   ................................................................................................................

   ................................................................................................................

6. Use the context to guess the meaning of *ephemeral* in this sentence from the passage: The Web may seem ephemeral, but what you casually post one night might just last a digital eternity.

   ................................................................................................................

7. Based on your reading of "Web of Risks," what are the concerns that some adults have about social networking sites? List as many as you can below. You will use these later for your research paper.

   ................................................................................................................

   ................................................................................................................

   ................................................................................................................

   ................................................................................................................

   ................................................................................................................

**Now answer this question with a partner.**

How well did your notes help you answer the comprehension questions? Go back to the reading and revise your notes, if necessary.

## 8 Critical Analysis

**In small groups, discuss your answers to the following questions.**

Compare the use of social networking sites by boys and girls. What are the differences? Why might girls use social networking sites more than boys? Why might boys use them differently than girls?

## 9 Vocabulary in Context

**There are several verb + noun collocations in "Social Networking Sites and Teens" and "Web of Risks." Find each of the following collocations and try to guess the meaning from the context.**

1. stay in touch ................................................................................................

2. see in person ................................................................................................

3. learn the hard way ................................................................................................

4. post online ................................................................................................

5. get into trouble ................................................................................................

6. take notice ................................................................................................

## 10 Vocabulary in Context

For each of the underlined words in the following sentences from "Social Networking Sites and Teens" (1) and "Web of Risks" (2), choose the best definition from the list below. Write the number of the sentence next to the definition.

1. In the past five years, such sites have rocketed from a niche activity into a phenomenon that engages tens of millions of Internet users. (1)

2. The explosive growth in the popularity of these sites has generated concerns among some parents, school officials, and government leaders about the potential risks posed to young people when personal information is made available in such a public setting. (1)

3. We define social networking Web sites here as sites where users can create a profile and connect that profile to other profiles for the purposes of making an explicit personal network. (1)

4. Though Walker claimed he was trying only to expose the guard's demeanor, he was expelled. (2)

5. A student's personal Facebook page is usually a revealing, dynamic chronicle of campus life—one clearly not meant for the eyes of parents, teachers, or anyone else older than 25. (2)

6. A student's personal Facebook page is usually a revealing, dynamic chronicle of campus life—one clearly not meant for the eyes of parents, teachers, or anyone else older than 25. (2)

7. The results can be awkward—or worse. Photos from drunken parties, recollections of sexual escapades, profanity, or threats—all these indiscretions, posted online, have gotten students suspended or expelled or have harmed job prospects. (2)

8. Harvard student Marc Zuckerberg and a few classmates designed Facebook in 2003 to facilitate contact among students. (2)

### Definitions

.............. **a.** clear; not hiding anything

.............. **b.** a thing that is remarkable or very unusual

.............. **c.** possible

.............. **d.** full of energy

.............. **e.** to make the truth about something known to the public

.............. **f.** to make something easier

.............. **g.** chances of being successful

.............. **h.** allowing something previously unknown to be known

## 11 Writing a Summary

Write a one-paragraph summary of "Web of Risks."

# Reading 2

## 1 Previewing

Preview the reading on pages 180 to 183. Look at the title. Then read the first paragraph, the last paragraph, and the headings.

## 2 Thinking about the Topic

In small groups, discuss your answers to the following questions.

1. Do you have an account with a networking Web site such as MySpace or Facebook? If so, explain how you use it.

2. Are you concerned about privacy on the Internet? Explain your answer.

3. What are some ways that people can avoid having their privacy invaded on the Internet?

## 3 Making Predictions

In small groups, discuss your answers to the following questions.

1. What do you think *paradox* means?

2. What do you think is the main idea of "A Privacy Paradox"?

3. What details or examples might the author include to develop the main idea?

## 4 Taking Notes for a Research Paper

Now read the text. Take notes as you read. Use index cards or pieces of paper for the facts that you want to record.

# A Privacy Paradox

In America, we live in a paradoxical world of privacy. While American adults are concerned about how the government and corporations are centrally collecting data about citizens and consumers, teenagers are freely giving up personal and private information in online journals. Marketers, school officials, government agencies, and online predators can collect data about young people through online teenage diaries. Herein lies the privacy paradox. Adults are concerned about invasion of privacy, while teens freely give up personal information. This occurs because often teens are not aware of the public nature of the Internet.

## The Public Nature of the Internet

The private versus public boundaries of social media spaces are unclear. On the Internet, the illusion of privacy creates boundary problems. According to Katz and Rice (2002), new users tend to feel this illusion the most. Some of the confusion about the public versus private space associated with social networks arises with the sign-up procedure. Sullivan (2005) maintains that "the sites deserve some blame for the release of personal information. In the sign-up process, many ask for e-mail addresses, for example" (para. 24). Asking for this type of information and setting up requirements for membership tend to make kids think it is safe to reveal personal information online. Friendster has a registration process, and LinkedIn is for people with professional affiliations. Additionally, Facebook requires an affiliation with a college or high school, which also creates the idea of a semiprivate space. Sitting at home alone typing into a computer may feel like a private exchange. However, once private information is posted on the Internet, it becomes available for others to read. We have no control over who can read our seemingly private words.

## Privacy Issues

Etzioni (1999) argues that the first step in examining a privacy issue is to determine whether or not there is a problem. Do we have a problem with the sharing of private information on social networking sites? According to the popular press and recent reports, there are a number of social concerns associated with social networking sites including the following: teenagers revealing too much information about themselves online (Bahrampour & Aratani, 2006; Downes, 2006; Komblum, 2005; Sullivan, 2005; Viser, 2005); children being exposed to pedophiles (Huffaker & Calvert, 2005; Lenhart, 2005); teenagers being raped by people they meet on social networking sites (Antone, 2006; Associated Press, 2006a; Reuters, 2006b); companies using the sites to collect marketing information (Hempel & Lehman, 2005; Verini, 2006); and children under the age of 14 using social networks (Antone, 2006; Reuters, 2006b). As reported in Reuters, "Under-14s are not supposed to use MySpace but tens of thousands ignore that stipulation, inventing ages and high school careers still beyond their reach, and sometimes posting sexually preco-cious pictures" (para. 15).

According to three 2005 Pew reports (Lenhart, 2005 Lenhart et al., 2005; Lenhart & Madden, 2005), 87 percent of American teens aged 12–17 are using the Internet. Fifty-one percent of these teenagers state that they go online on a daily basis. Approximately four million teenagers, or 19 percent, say that they create their own Weblogs (personal online journals), and 22 percent report that they maintain a personal Web page (Lenhart & Madden, 2005). In blogs and on personal Web sites, teenagers are providing so much personal information about themselves that it has become a concern. Today, content creation means sharing not only music and videos but also personal diaries.

An analysis of Weblogs showed that the types of personal information revealed online include name; address; birth date; location; and numerous types of online contact information, including e-mail addresses, instant messaging user names, and links to personal Web pages (Huffaker & Calvert, 2005). According to Huffaker and Calvert (2005), "Because teenage bloggers are revealing a considerable amount of personal information, as well as multiple ways to contact them online, the danger of cyberstalking and communicating with strangers online is a serious issue" (para. 63).

Marketers who target teen consumers can use stated personal information gathered from social networking sites for purposes other than what users intend. Today, the commoditization of information has made it necessary to consider the invasion of privacy by corporations. Schement and Curtis (1995) state that "information is gathered so that the economy can support its participants" (p. 137). In a capitalistic society, marketers can use personal information collected from public online databases for commercial purposes. Additionally, companies such as Coke, Apple Computer, and Procter & Gamble are using social networking sites as promotional tools. For instance, Apple Computer sponsors the Apple discussion list on Facebook.

Schools can also access and use the information posted on social networking sites. At Chicago's Loyola University, athletes were told to get off Facebook and MySpace or risk losing their scholarships (*Sports Illustrated*, 2006). In May 2006, a number of hazing photos appeared on a site called badjocks.com showing athletes from Princeton University, the University of Michigan, Fordham University, and the University of California at Santa Barbara behaving badly. As a result, schools have started investigations into student athlete behavior.

**Privacy Solutions**

Solutions to protecting privacy at online social networking sites can be approached in three different ways—social solutions, technical solutions, and legal solutions. Parents, schools, and social networking sites are working on various social solutions to the privacy problem. Experts (Sullivan, 2005) agree that the first step in building protections for teenage bloggers starts with parents. A representative from Wired Safety.org remarked (as cited in Sullivan, 2005) that "parents need to be much more involved with their kids' computer use than they are" (para. 26). A growing gap is evolving between teenage and parent use of new technology, and parents need to spend time learning about these differences. Downes (2006) points out that "The Federal Bureau of Investigation and the National Center for Missing and Exploited Children offer parents advice for detecting whether their child is engaging in appropriate behavior" (para. 8).

Schools have also taken action to protect the safety of young individuals in social networking sites, and they are scrambling to come up with policies on social networking sites. As Jenkins and Boyd (2006) report, "In many cases, schools are being forced to respond to real world problems which only came to their attention because this information was so publicly accessible on the Web" (para. 10). But schools are not clear about what actions they should take about student participation in social networking sites.

Principals have called, written, and sent e-mail to parents about teens placing too much personal information on the Internet. Some schools have banned blogs and have asked students to take their information off the network (Kornblum, 2005). Other schools have refused to let students register for social networking sites with a school e-mail address. Additionally, Bahrampour and Aratani (2006) report that schools are warning students that college admissions officers and future employers are checking social networking sites to read what applicants have written online. Colleges and universities have taken action as a result of hazing photographs of athletes appearing on the Internet. Teams have been suspended, and student athletes are requested to take their images off the Internet. Additionally, students are being warned that they will be reprimanded for pictures posted on the Internet that reveal misbehavior (Wolverton, 2006).

Currently, commercial social networking companies are reacting to the problem of teens online. MySpace has reported "working with the National Center for Missing and Exploited Children and the Advertising Council to create the largest-ever online safety program using nationwide public service advertisements" (Auchard, 2006). MySpace is posting safety ads. These appear as banner ads at the top of MySpace pages.

In addition to social awareness, social networking sites are exploring technological solutions to better protect their users. As Duffy (2006) states, "A few cases of online friendships that turned violent or even homicidal have pressured social-network sites to provide better security for their members. Facebook recently overhauled its privacy setting to give members tighter controls over who sees what" (para. 6). Additionally, MySpace utilizes software to try to identify children under the age of 14. But they admitted that it was difficult to verify the ages of all their users (Reuters, 2006a). As a result, Massachusetts Attorney General Tom Reilly "asked MySpace to install an age and identity verification system, equip Web pages with a 'Report Inappropriate Content' link, respond to all reports of inappropriate content within 24 hours, and significantly raise the number of staff who review images and content" (para. 15).

Legal solutions to privacy issues involve both the human monitoring of social networking sites and technological solutions. On May 10, 2006, Representative Michael Fitzpatrick, a Pennsylvania Republican, introduced a new bill into Congress. It is called the Deleting Online Predators Act (DOPA). Jenkins and Boyd (2006) point out that DOPA "is so broadly defined that it would limit access to any commercial site that allows users to create a profile and communicate with strangers" (para. 22). Although this bill would help to protect teens who access social networking sites through libraries and schools, it would not protect teens using computers in their own homes. Protection of teens is a parental responsibility. But the education of teens and their parents to the growing privacy problem will require an effort that involves schools, social networking organizations, and government agencies.

## Conclusion

The solution to the paradox is not simple. It will take all levels of society to tackle the social issues related to teens and privacy. Awareness is key to solving the solution. We as individuals need to be more proactive about educating each other and protecting our privacy on the Internet.

## References

Antone, R. (2006, March 9). Another isle man allegedly baits teen victim on MySpace. *Honolulu Star Bulletin*. Retrieved March 21, 2006, from http://starbulletin.com/2006/03/09/news/story05.html

Associated Press. (2006a, February 3). Police: Teens may have met assailants on MySpace.com. *CNN.com*. Retrieved February 21, 2006, from http://www.cnn.com/2006/TECH/internet/02/03/myspace.assaults.ap/index.html

Bahrampour, T., & Aratani, L. (2006, January 17). Teens' bold blogs alarm area schools. *Washington Post*. Retrieved January 18, 2006, from http://www.washingtonpost.com/wpdyn/content/article/2006/01/16/AR2006011601489.html

Downes, S. (2006, January 15). Teens who tell too much. *New York Times*. Retrieved January 18, 2006, from http://www.nytimes.com/

Duffy, M. (2006, March 19). A dad's encounter with the vortex of Facebook. *Time*. Retrieved March 21, 2006, from http://www.time.com/time/magazine/article/0,9171,1174704,00.html

Etzioni, A. (1999). *The limits of privacy*. New York: Basic Books.

Hempel, J., & Lehman, P. (2005, December 12). The MySpace generation. *BusinessWeek*. Retrieved December 8, 2005, from http://www.businessweek.com/

Huffaker, D. A., & Calvert, S. L. (2005). Gender, identity, and language use in teenage blogs. Journal of Computer–Mediated Communication, volume 10, number 2. Retrieved April 6, 2005, from http://jcmc.indiana.edu/vol10/issue2/huffaker.html

Jenkins, H., & Boyd, D. (2006, May 24). Discussion: MySpace and Deleting Online Predators Act (DOPA). *MIT Tech Talk*. Retrieved May 26, 2006, from http://www.danah.org/papers/MySpaceDOPA.html

Katz, J. E., & Rice, R. E. (2002). *Social consequences of Internet use: Access, involvement, and interaction*. Cambridge, Mass: MIT Press.

Kornblum, J. (2005, October 30). Teens wear their hearts on their blog. *USA Today*. Retrieved November 1, 2005, from http://www.usatoday.com/tech/news/techinnovations/2005-10-30-teen-blogs_x.htm

Lenhart, A. (2005). Protecting teens online. *Pew Internet & American Life Project*. Retrieved March 14, 2005, from http://www.pewinternet.org/pdfs/PIP_Filters_Report.pdf

Lenhart, A., & Madden, M. (2005). Teen content creators and consumers. *Pew Internet & American Life Project*. Retrieved March 14, 2005, from http://www.pewinternet.org/pdfs/PIP_Teens_Content_Creatio.pdf

Lenhart, A., Madden, M., & Hitlin, P. (2005). Teens and technology: Youth are leading the transition to a fully wired and mobile nation. *Pew Internet & American Life Project*. Retrieved March 14, 2005, from http://www.pewinternet.org/PPF/r/162/report_display.asp

Reuters. (2006a, May 3). State wants My Space to raise minimum age. Retrieved August 20, 2006, from http://www.rapidnew-swire.com/5036-myspace-0245.htm

Reuters. (2006b, May 11). As freedom shrinks, teens seek MySpace to hang out. Retrieved August 20, 2006, from http://today.reuters.com/news/articlebusiness.aspx?type=media&storyID=nN09287157&from=business

Schement, J. R., & Curtis, T. (1995). *Tendencies and tensions of the information age: The production and distribution of information in the United States*. New Brunswick, N.J.: Transaction Publishers.

*Sports Illustrated*. (2006, May 26). Blogs, photo sites give everyone a peek at athletes' lives. Retrieved May 26, 2006, from http://www.si.com

Sullivan, B. (2005). Kids, blogs and too much information: Children reveal more online than parents know. *MSNBC.com*. Retrieved March 21, 2006, from http://www.msnbc.msn.com/id/7668788/print/1/displaymode/1098/

Verini, J. (2006, March). Will success spoil MySpace? [electronic version]. *Vanity Fair*, 238–249.

Viser, M. (2005, December 8). Website's power to overexpose teens stirs a warning. *Boston Globe*. Retrieved December 8, 2005, from http://www.boston.com/business/personaltech/articles/2005/12/08/websites_power_to_overexpose_teens_stirs_a_warning/

Wolverton, B. (2006, June 2). Hazing photos spur debates on complicity of coaches: Athletics officials suspend teams and restrict sharing of pictures on the Internet [electronic version]. *Chronicle of Higher Education*, A1, A33–34.

### Source Information

Title of Article: "A Privacy Paradox"

Author: Susan B. Barnes

Publication: *First Monday*

Date/Issue: volume 11, number 9 (September 2006).

URL: http://firstmonday.org/issues/issue11_9/barnes/index.html

## 5 Comparing Notes

**Compare your notes with a partner and answer the following questions.**

As you read "A Privacy Paradox," what information seemed useful? What did you take notes on? Did you miss anything that your partner noticed? Revise your notes, if necessary.

## 6 Comprehension Check

**Write your answers to the following questions. Try to use your notes.**

1. What is the author's main point in this article?

   ..............................................................................................................................

   ..............................................................................................................................

2. Why do some kids tend to think that social networking sites are safer than they really are?

   ..............................................................................................................................

   ..............................................................................................................................

3. What type of information did Huffaker and Calvert's 2005 analysis of Weblogs reveal? (para. 5)

   ..............................................................................................................................

   ..............................................................................................................................

4. How do large corporations use social networking sites?

   ..............................................................................................................................

5. What are some of the concerns about privacy and social networking sites, as referred to by the author? Match concerns with the authors of various studies and/or reports. (para. 3)

| Author(s) of Study/Report | Concerns |
|---|---|
| Bahrampour & Aratani, 2006; Downes, 2006; Komblum, 2005; Sullivan, 2005; Viser, 2005 | |
| Huffaker & Calvert, 2005; Lenhart, 2005 | |
| Antone, 2006; Associated Press, 2006a; Reuters, 2006b | |
| Hempel & Lehman, 2005; Verini, 2006 | |
| Antone, 2006; Reuters, 2006b | |

**6.** What three types of solutions to privacy concerns are there, according to this article?

........................................................................................................................................................

**7.** Write a one-paragraph summary of the solutions to privacy concerns referred to in the article.

**Now answer this question with a partner.**

How well did your notes help you answer the comprehension questions? Go back to the reading and revise your notes, if necessary.

## 7   Critical Analysis

**In small groups, discuss your answers to the following questions.**

How old should children be before they are allowed to use the Internet? How old should they be before they are allowed to use social networking sites? What restrictions, if any, should be placed on children who use the Internet and/or social networking sites?

**Reading ⟶ *Analyzing a Problem-Solution Passage***

A problem-solution passage presents a problem and suggests solutions to the problem. It is one way of developing an argument. It often defines and/or gives background on an issue and then expresses concerns regarding the issue. It may present one way to alleviate the problem or several.

## 8   Analyzing a Problem-Solution Passage

**Answer these questions about "A Privacy Paradox."**

**1.** What is the author's thesis statement? Where does she express it?

**2.** In which paragraphs does she define and/or give background on the issues?

**3.** In which paragraphs does the author define the problem(s)?

**4.** In which paragraphs does she offer solutions to the problem(s)?

**5.** What does the author say in her conclusion?

**6.** Make a map or an outline the shows the organization of ideas in "A Privacy Paradox." Make your own or complete the following map.

**1: Introduction**

Purpose:_____

_____

Thesis statement :_____

_____

↓

**2: The Public Nature of the Internet**

Purpose:_____

_____

↓

**3: Privacy Issues**

Purpose:_____

_____

↓

**4: Privacy Solutions**

Purpose:_____

_____

↓

**5: Conclusion**

Purpose:_____

_____

## 9　Vocabulary in Context

Scan the article for the verbs listed below and underline them. Then, using the context provided by the article and a dictionary, match the verbs with the best definition.

............... 1.　to require (para. 2)　　　a.　to discover or find out something

............... 2.　to maintain (para. 4)　　　b.　to show

............... 3.　to reveal (para. 5)　　　　c.　to demand

............... 4.　to approach (para. 8)　　　d.　to deal with

............... 5.　to evolve (para. 8)　　　　e.　to continue to have

............... 6.　to detect (para. 8)　　　　f.　to come into being

............... 7.　to identify (para. 12)　　　g.　to provide

............... 8.　to equip (para. 12)　　　　h.　to point out

## Vocabulary → *Recognizing and Using Lead-in Expressions*

The author of "A Privacy Paradox" bases her discussion of the privacy issues related to online social networks on research findings. The use of research to support and develop one's ideas is a fundamental element of academic writing. References to research strengthen writing and demonstrate that the writer has a strong basis for his or her point of view.

It is essential to give credit to the researchers whose work you are using. A writer who does so is sure to avoid plagiarism. (Review Chapter 4 for more information on plagiarism.) In addition, giving credit allows readers to find the studies or related articles if they want to read them for themselves. It also demonstrates that the writer is honest and is not trying to take credit for work or ideas that are not his or her own.

One of the techniques for naming the sources of your information is using **lead-in expressions** to introduce the authors of a study. These are integrated into the body of the text. Study the following lead-ins from "A Privacy Paradox":

LEAD-IN: *according to X*

EXAMPLE: <u>According to</u> Katz and Rice (2002), new users tend to feel this illusion the most.

LEAD-IN: *X report that*

EXAMPLE: Additionally, Bahrampour and Aratani (2006) <u>report that</u> schools are warning students that college admissions officers and future employers are checking social networking sites to read what applicants have written online.

### More Lead-in Expressions

Other lead-in strategies can also be used to introduce authors and their ideas. Study the following lead-ins and examples:

**1.** For problems, questions, or issues

*X discusses* + a problem, a question, or an issue
*X examines* + a problem, a question, or an issue
*X addresses* + a problem, a question, or an issue

EXAMPLE: Barnes <u>discusses</u> privacy issues related to online networking sites.

**2.** For suggestions

*X recommends* + a suggestion
*X suggests* + a suggestion
*X proposes* + a suggestion

EXAMPLE: Barnes <u>proposes</u> three types of solutions to online networking privacy issues.

**3.** For opinions

*X believes* + an opinion
*X contends* + an opinion
*X posits* + an opinion
*X claims* + an opinion
*X argues* + an opinion
*X maintains* + an opinion

EXAMPLE: Barnes <u>believes that</u> the solution to the privacy problem is not simple.

**4.** For original insights or ideas presented by the author
*X points out* + an original insight or idea

EXAMPLE: Barnes <u>points out that</u> teens are often not aware of the public nature of the Internet.

NOTE: If something is *pointed out*, it must exist or be true.

## 10 Using Lead-in Expressions

Paraphrase the information in the chart you completed in Activity 6, item 5, on page 184 using appropriate lead-ins from the box above. Or paraphrase the findings of Barnes, the author of "A Privacy Paradox."

# The Research Paper

### Documenting Information

To avoid plagiarism and to give credit to the writers whose work they are using, academic writers also include bibliographic information. This helps the reader find the books and articles that were used to write the academic text. When writers include this bibliographic information, they are **documenting information**.

There are several different styles for documenting information. These include APA (American Psychological Association), MLA (Modern Language Association), Turabian, and Chicago. You should find out what documentation style is used in your field. The APA and the MLA styles are illustrated below.

#### APA

APA uses an author-date system. The name of the author and the date of publication are integrated into the body of the text. Page or paragraph numbers* are included when material is quoted or a specific detail is given from the original source. Readers can then look up the authors' names in a reference list, where they will find the rest of the publication information.

  *NOTE: You give the paragraph number for material on Web sites that may not have a page number.

#### MLA

MLA uses an author-page number system. The name of the author and the page or paragraph number of the information or idea within the original source are integrated into the body of the text. The reader can then look up the authors' names in a reference list, where they will find the rest of the publication information.

#### In-Text Citations That Mention the Author in the Lead-In

*   APA

    Barnes (2006) suggests that the protection of teens is a parental responsibility.
    ‾‾‾‾‾‾   ‾‾‾‾
    Author     Date

*   MLA

    According to Tomkins, Gehry first makes a model that follows his clients' specifications and
    ‾‾‾‾‾‾‾
    Author

    then experiments with it (41).
    ‾‾‾‾
    Page

#### In-Text Citations That Do Not Mention the Author in the Lead-In

*   APA

    Older teen girls are more likely to have used social networking sites than boys in the same
    age group (Lenhart & Madden, 2007).
    ‾‾‾‾‾‾‾‾‾‾‾‾‾‾‾  ‾‾‾‾
    Source                 Date

*   MLA

    Relaxed standards of dress are a good example of the shift in attitude from pleasing others
    to pleasing oneself (Twenge 18).
    ‾‾‾‾‾  ‾‾
    Source   Page

**Citing Short Quotations in the Text**

- APA

  Jenkins and Boyd (2006) point out that DOPA "is so broadly defined that it would limit
  <sub>Author</sub>        <sub>Date</sub>

  access to any commercial site that allows users to create a profile and communicate with
  strangers" (para. 22).
  <sub>Paragraph</sub>

- MLA

  In describing it, McGuigan writes, "The quay, once abandoned to warehouses and freight
  <sub>Author</sub>

  cars, has come to life with a long outside staircase (The Fred-and-Ginger stairway, Gehry
  calls it) swooping down to the water" (69).
  <sub>Page</sub>

## 1 Analyzing a Model of Documenting Sources

**Work with a partner to analyze "A Privacy Paradox" on pages 180 to 183.**

1. Which style does "A Privacy Paradox" follow, APA or MLA?

2. Find two examples of in-text citations that mention the author in the lead-in.

3. Find two examples of in-text citations that don't mention the author in the lead-in.

4. Find two examples of short quotations cited in the text.

5. Where did the author probably find the following material? How do you know?

   Jenkins and Boyd (2006) point out that DOPA "is so broadly defined that it
   would limit access to any commercial site that allows users to create a profile and
   communicate with strangers" (para. 22).

## 2 Documenting Citing Sources in a Research Paper

**Go back to Activity 10 on page 188. Using either APA style or MLA style, add
documentation information to your paraphrases.**

## Reference List

Writers must also provide a reference list so that their readers can find the complete publication information. The reference list must follow the specific conventions of the documentation style chosen by the writer; for example, if the writer has referenced information in the body of the paper using APA style, the reference list at the end of the paper must also follow the conventions of APA. Here are examples of several types of references.

### Book

- **APA**

  Baker, R. K., & Ball, S. J. (1969). *Mass media and violence* (Vol. 9). Washington D.C.:
  Authors         Date     Title                     Place of Publication

  United States Government Printing Office.
  Publisher

- **MLA**

  Hawkes, Lory. *A Guide to the World Wide Web*. Upper Saddle River, New Jersey:
  Author                Title                 Place of Publication

  Prentice Hall, 1999.
  Publisher      Date

### Journal or Magazine Article

- **APA**

  Waters, H. F., & Malamud, P. (1975). Drop that gun, Captain Video!
  Authors                  Date       Article Title

  *Newsweek*, 85(10), 81–82.
  Magazine Title Vol. No. (Is. No.) Pages

- **MLA**

  Vandrick, Stephanie. "Diaspora Literature: A Mirror for ESL Students."
  Author                          Article Title

  *College ESL 7.2* (1997): 25–27.
  Magazine Title Vol. No.  (Year)     Pages

### Internet

Documentation of online sources is evolving. For that reason, the methods of documentation may vary. However, what is important is that, if you use online sources, you give your readers as much access information as possible so that they can find the sources. It is important to give the name(s) of the author(s), the title of the document, the publication date, the date of access, and the path followed to locate the source. Two styles are shown here.

- **APA**

  Hempel, J., & Lehman, P. (2005, December 12). The MySpace generation. *BusinessWeek*. Retrieved December 8, 2005, from http://www.businessweek.com/

- **MLA**

  CRTC Public Affairs. Canada & TV Violence: Cooperation and Consensus. 14 March 1996. 1 March 1999. <http://www.crtc.gc.ca/eng/social/violarte.htm>.
  Date Retrieved         Note: Carets [< >] around URL

### Formatting a Reference List

When writing a reference list for a college paper, you always double-space your list (as you do your entire paper). You also indent by one-half inch every line in each entry except for the first line.

Example:

Hempel, J., & Lehman, P. (2005, December 12). The MySpace generation. *BusinessWeek*. Retrieved December 8, 2005, from http://www.businessweek.com/

## 3 Documenting Sources in a Reference List

**1. Revise the bibliographic entries below so that they are consistent with either APA or MLA guidelines. (Note: Be sure to examine the punctuation carefully.) Refer to the model references presented above. Use today's date for the retrieval date of the Internet entry. Put the entries in alphabetical order.**

Josephson, Wendy L. Television Violence: A Review of the Effects on Children of Different Ages. February, 1995. Ottawa: National Clearinghouse on Family Violence.

*A Textbook of Social Psychology* (3rd ed.). by J. E. Alcock, D. W. Carment, & S. W. Sadava. 1994. Scarborough: Prentice Hall Canada Inc.

"Boob-tubed Imaginations" in *Equinox* by Bruce McDougall. Volume 8, Number 1, Jan./Feb., 1989. 28, 31.

Chidley, Joe. "Toxic TV" in *Maclean's*. Volume 109, June 17, 1996. 36–41.

"Privacy for Internet Names Moves Forward," by Anick Jesdanun. March 20, 2006. Associated Press. http://apnews.excite.com/article/20070320/D8O03I980.html

**2. Rewrite the source information on your note cards so that it is consistent with either APA or MLA guidelines. Add a correct source note for "Social Networking Sites and Teens," pages 172 to 173. Use today's date for any website retrievals. Put them in alphabetical order.**

# Reading 3

## 1 Previewing

Preview the reading on pages 193 to 194. Look at the title. Then read the introductory paragraph that follows the title and the last paragraph. Scan the bold questions.

## 2 Thinking about the Topic

In small groups, discuss your answers to the following questions.

1. Review some of the solutions to the concerns about Internet privacy that you read about in "A Privacy Paradox." Can you think of others? If so, explain them.

2. What should parents do to keep their children safe on the Internet?

3. From what you read about DOPA in "A Privacy Paradox" (para. 13), do you think it is a useful solution to some to the dangers children face on the Internet?

## 3 Making Predictions

In small groups, discuss your answers to the following questions.

1. What type of passage is this? What do the questions in bold type indicate?

2. What do you think is the main idea of this reading?

3. What details or examples might the interviewer and the interviewees include to develop the main idea?

## 4 Taking Notes for a Research Paper

Now read the text. Take notes as you read. Use index cards or pieces of paper for the facts that you want to record. This time, make sure that your reference citation follows the correct format.

# Discussion: MySpace and DOPA

*The following is an excerpt from an interview with Henry Jenkins (co-director of the Comparative Media Studies Program at MIT) and Danah Boyd (PhD student at the School of Information, University of California at Berkeley) that was conducted via e-mail by Sarah Wright of the MIT News Office.*

**What is MySpace, and what is the controversy over it?**

**Boyd:** Structurally, social network sites are a cross between a yearbook and a community Web site. MySpace is a social network site where individuals create digital profiles and link to others ("friends") within the system—similar to sharing home pages.

While MySpace allows 14- and 15-year-old users to restrict who can see their page and contact them, most users opt to make their profiles public. The primary concern is that this openness puts youth at risk, making them particularly vulnerable to predators.

**Jenkins:** More broadly, teens and adults have developed different notions of privacy: young people feel relatively comfortable sharing aspects of their lives (for example, their sexual identities). In some cases, teens do not fully understand the risks of making certain information public.

**What do "social networking software programs" provide participants?**

**Boyd:** By giving youth access to a public of their peers, MySpace provides a fertile ground for identity development and cultural integration. Youth view MySpace as a place where they can be who they are, joke around with friends, and make certain to stay in the loop about everything that is going on around them.

**What would be the effect of the proposed legislation on youth?**

**Boyd:** This legislation is targeting MySpace, but it would also block blogging tools, mailing lists, video and podcast sites, photo-sharing sites, and educational sites like NeoPets. So it would extend current regulations that require all federally funded schools and libraries to deploy Internet filters. The law is so broadly defined that it would limit access to any commercial site that allows users to create a profile and communicate with strangers.

**What about the deterrent effect on predators?**

**Boyd:** Unfortunately, predators lurk wherever youth hang out. Since youth are on MySpace, there are bound to be predators on MySpace. Yet, fewer than .01 percent of all youth abductions nationwide are stranger abductions: youth are at far greater risk of abuse in their own homes and in the homes of their friends than they ever are in digital or physical publics. Also, police currently patrol MySpace, just as they patrol other areas where youth hang out. Many are thankful to know where youth go online because it helps them do their job.

**You have previously compared virtual socializing to the free play in the backyards of 1950s America. Have new media changed the nature of play?**

**Jenkins:** What teens are doing online is no better and no worse than what previous generations of teens did when their parents weren't looking. The difference is that as these activities are being digitized, they are also being brought into public view. Parents are experiencing this as a loss of control, but in fact, adults have greater control over these aspects of their children's lives than ever before.

One of the biggest risks of these digital technologies is not the ways that they allow teens to escape adult control but rather the permanent traces left behind of their transgressive conduct.

**Boyd:** While integrating into cultural life is critical during these years, the actual process is not always smooth or pleasant. Bullying, sexual teasing, and other peer-to-peer harassment are rampant among teenagers. MySpace did not create teenage bullying, but it has made it more visible to many adults. This visibility can provide a window through which teen mentors can help combat this issue.

**What suggestions do you have for parents eager to help their children cope with online social networks?**

**Henry:** Parents face serious challenges in helping their children negotiate through these new online environments. They receive very little advice about how to build a constructive relationship with media within their families or how to help their offspring make ethical choices as participants in these online worlds.

Recognizing that different parents will approach these issues in different ways, we would still offer the following as our governing philosophy for dealing with MySpace and other social software.

**1.** Communication with your daughter or son is key. Build a trusting relationship through dialogue. It is important to talk with [your kids] about your concerns; it is even more important to listen to what they have to say about their online experiences and why these sites are such an important part of their interactions with their peers. You need to recognize that some unfamiliar experiences look scarier from the outside than they are. Take time to understand what you are seeing and what it means to participants.

**2.** Create an account to understand how the site works, but not to stalk your kids. They need room to explore, but if you are familiar with the media and technology that they consume, you can provide valuable guidance and suggestions. Surveillance, while possible, damages a trusting parent/child relationship.

**3.** Ask your kids how they choose to represent themselves and why. Use MySpace as a resource to start a conversation about contemporary fashion, ideals, and media images.

**4.** Talk about private/public issues with your kids. Help them to understand the consequences of making certain information publicly accessible. Get them to think through all of the possible audiences who might come into contact with their online information. Teens often imagine MySpace as a youth-only world. It isn't, and they need to consider what the consequences would be if their grandparents, their teachers, admissions officers, or a future employer read what they said about themselves. Helping your children learn how to negotiate such public environments is a great educational opportunity.

**5.** Talk through what kids should do if they receive unwanted attention online or if they find themselves the victims of cyberbullying. A growing number of sites provide useful information about how to confront such problems, including Net Family News, NetSmartz, and SafeTeens. The "Safety Tips" section of MySpace also provides information for both parents and teens, including MySpace policies.

---

**Source Information**

Title of Article: "Discussion: MySpace and DOPA"

Interviewees: Danah Boyd and Henry Jenkins

Publication: *MIT Tech Talk*

Date: May 26, 2006

URL: http://www.danah.org/papers/MySpaceDOPA.html

## 5  Comparing Notes

**Compare your notes with a partner and answer the following questions.**

As you read "Discussion: MySpace and DOPA," what information seemed useful? What did you take notes on? Did you miss anything that your partner noticed? Revise your notes, if necessary.

## 6  Comprehension Check

**Write your answers to the following questions. Try to use your notes.**

1. How does Boyd describe MySpace?

   ...........................................................................................................................

   ...........................................................................................................................

2. Restate Boyd and Jenkins's explanation of the controversy over MySpace. (paras. 1–3)

   ...........................................................................................................................

   ...........................................................................................................................

3. What do social networking sites provide young people, according to Boyd?

   ...........................................................................................................................

4. Does Boyd believe that DOPA is the solution to keeping young people safe from predators on the Internet? Explain your answer.

   ...........................................................................................................................

   ...........................................................................................................................

5. Summarize in your own words Jenkins's five suggestions for parents who want to help their children cope with social networking sites.

   ...........................................................................................................................

   ...........................................................................................................................

   ...........................................................................................................................

   ...........................................................................................................................

**Now answer this question with a partner.**

How well did your notes help you answer the comprehension questions? Go back to the reading and revise your notes, if necessary.

### Critical Analysis ⟶ *Synthesizing Information*

**Synthesizing information** is a kind of critical analysis. When you synthesize information, you combine and unify ideas from different sources. This is useful when you need to formulate a point of view and select reasons and evidence to support your opinions.

## 7 Critical Analysis: Synthesizing Information

**Using information from all the passages in this chapter, discuss your answers to the following questions. Work in small groups.**

1. Considering the results of the survey reported on in "Social Networking Sites and Teens," whom might DOPA be more likely to protect from an online predator, a girl or a boy? Why?

2. How would the author of "A Privacy Paradox" characterize college student Brad Davis ("Web of Risks")?

3. Apply Jenkins's suggestions for parents to the teens described in the survey reported on in "Social Networking Sites and Teens" and to the college students in "Web of Risks." How appropriate are they for each group?

4. How might Mark Zuckerberg ("Web of Risks") feel about DOPA as described in "A Privacy Paradox"?

## 8 Vocabulary in Context

**Skim the interview for the words listed below. As you find each word, think about possible meanings for it. Use the sentences that follow to help determine the meaning. (You may also use a dictionary.) Write the definitions on the lines.**

| | |
|---|---|
| notions (para. 3) | visible (para. 9) |
| targeting (para. 5) | constructive (para. 10) |
| traces (para. 8) | philosophy (para. 11) |
| integrating (para. 9) | consume (para. 13) |

1. The new ad is targeting teens, but the company is hoping that parents will see it as well.

Meaning: _____

2. The senator's philosophy about protecting kids online is strict: he believes that all access should be denied to anyone under age 12.

Meaning: _____

3. Some parents have very unrealistic notions about what really goes on online; others have a pretty clear idea of what their children are doing.

Meaning: _____

4. Online activities consume an average of five hours a day for some children, while other children spend that amount of time in active play.

Meaning: _____

5. Jack hasn't gotten along with his parents for a long time, but now, thanks to therapy, they've manage to create a constructive relationship.

Meaning: _____

**6.** Before, people weren't paying attention to the role MySpace was playing in young people lives; now, however, it has become quite <u>visible</u> to adults.

Meaning: _____

**7.** Jane came over to use my computer for several hours, but she must be a very neat person, because there are absolutely no <u>traces</u> of her ever being here.

Meaning: _____

**8.** In the past, teenagers become part of social groups at school; today, however, social networking sites are facilitating their social <u>integration</u>.

Meaning: _____

## 9 Synthesizing Information in Writing

**Write a one-paragraph response to one of the questions in Activity 7 above.**

# Writing Focus

## Writing a Research Paper

By now, you've gathered a great deal of information about the issues regarding online social networks. You've also thought about and discussed your own position on the positive and negative impact that social networking sites can have on teens and young adults.

You're ready to begin your research paper. You'll base it on your own perspective as well as the information that you have gathered in this chapter. A research paper is similar to an essay in terms of organization: it contains a thesis statement that is supported in the body of the paper. However, in drafting a research paper, you also use research findings to support and develop your own analysis of the topic.

### The Assignment

Use the information from at least three readings in this chapter to discuss the following question:

In several of the readings in this chapter, concerns about social networking sites are expressed. What are these concerns?
In your opinion, how can these concerns best be alleviated?

Present your argument in a paper of three to five pages.

## Determining Your Position

In an academic paper, it is very important to include your own ideas; in fact, after reading your paper, your readers should come away with a clear understanding of your own analysis of the topic. Therefore, it is important for you, as a writer, to clarify your own position.

One way to do this is to ask yourself questions about the material you've read on the topic so far. To what extent do you agree or disagree with issues? What are some alternative points of view? What else have you heard about these issues? Jot down any and all ideas without censoring them at this point.

## 1 Determining Your Position

To begin this research paper, think about the concerns about social network sites. Do you think they are legitimate? What do you think are the most effective ways of alleviating those concerns? On the lines below, write down your thoughts without censoring yourself or worrying about organization or grammar. Under each point, fill in any details or direct quotations from the articles that might help you develop each point. Use your note cards and include the source for the ideas or quotations as you write them in.

- What are the concerns related to online social networks?

.................................................................................................................

.................................................................................................................

.................................................................................................................

.................................................................................................................

.................................................................................................................

- In your opinion, how can these concerns be addressed most effectively?

.................................................................................................................

.................................................................................................................

.................................................................................................................

.................................................................................................................

.................................................................................................................

### Writing a Thesis Statement for a Research Paper

As in an essay, the thesis statement for a research paper expresses the main idea of your paper.

To write a thesis statement, think about your position in terms of the information that you have on the topic and ask yourself whether it will adequately support your position. If not, you can look for more supporting information, or you can revise your thesis.

## 2 Writing a Thesis Statement for a Research Paper

Activity 1 should have helped you formulate your own ideas on the topic. Now write a thesis statement for your research paper.

Thesis statement: ...................................................................................................

.................................................................................................................

## 3 Organizing Your Ideas

Review what you wrote in Activity 1 in light of your thesis statement. Discard any points that seem unimportant. Arrange the points in the order in which you will present them in your paper. This may be either from strongest to weakest or from weakest to strongest, depending on how you think the ideas best fit together.

## 4  Writing the First Draft

Now you're ready to write a first draft. First, think about your introduction. Consider what background information your reader might need in order to understand your thesis statement. Include this information in your introduction.

Write your first draft. Do not revise until you have completed your first draft. Make sure that you document your information as you write. Ask your teacher which style you should use.

## 5  After You Write

Answer the following questions about your essay.

1. Is the main argument of your paper clearly presented in the thesis statement?

2. Is the thesis statement directly related to the topic of the paper?

3. Did you support the thesis statement with relevant ideas in the body of the paper?

4. Are your supporting ideas introduced to your readers in clear topic sentences?

5. Have you used information from the readings to develop your supporting ideas?

6. Where could you add information to strengthen your argument?

7. Have you overused direct quotations? Remember, your paper should not be a stringing together of ideas from other authors. It should express your own analysis of the topic.

8. Did you give credit to the authors whose words and ideas you have used by using lead-ins and documentation?

## 6  The Second Draft

Now, revise your research paper and add a reference list to it. Use the source information on your note cards. Make sure the citations follow the correct format.

# Appendix

## Suffixes

| Suffix | Meaning | Part of Speech of Resulting Word |
|---|---|---|
| *-able, -ible* | capable of | adjective |
| *-ance, -ence* | instance of an action | noun |
| *-ation, -tion* | action or process | noun |
| *-er, -or* | person connected with | noun |
| *-ful* | full of | adjective |
| *-ic, -ical* | having the form of | adjective |
| *-ious, -ous* | having the qualities of | adjective |
| *-ish* | relating to | adjective |
| *-less* | not having | adjective |
| *-ly* | in the manner of | adverb |
| *-ness* | state or condition | noun |

## Prefixes

| Prefix | Meaning | Prefix | Meaning |
|---|---|---|---|
| *ante-* | before | *mis-* | wrongly |
| *anti-* | against | *mono-* | one |
| *bi-* | two | *multi-* | many |
| *circum-* | around | *non-* | not |
| *con-, co-, col-, com-* | with | *post-* | after |
| *counter-* | against | *pre-, prim-* | first or before |
| *de-* | opposite | *pro-* | for or before |
| *dis-* | opposite | *re-* | again |
| *ex-, e-* | out of, from | *semi-* | half |
| *hyper-* | above, excessively | *sub-, sup-* | under |
| *hypo-* | under, below | *trans-* | across or beyond |
| *inter-* | between | *tri-* | three |
| *intra-* | within | *un-, im-, in-* | no, not |
| *macro-* | small | | |

# Vocabulary Index

## Chapter 1

| | |
|---|---|
| after | 16 |
| also | 7 |
| alter | 3 |
| although | 16 |
| because | 16 |
| before | 16 |
| challenge | 11 |
| consequently | 9 |
| crucial | 12 |
| culture | 11 |
| despite | 7 |
| distribution | 4 |
| diversity | 3 |
| estimated | 18 |
| even though | 16 |
| financial | 3 |
| first | 7 |
| focus | 11 |
| for example | 3 |
| for instance | 7 |
| for these reasons | 7 |
| function | 3 |
| furthermore | 3 |
| however | 3 |
| in brief | 7 |
| in conclusion | 7 |
| in summary | 7 |
| inappropriate | 19 |
| liberalized | 3 |
| likewise | 7 |
| maintaining | 11 |
| moreover | 4 |
| nevertheless | 3 |
| next | 7 |
| on the other hand | 7 |
| option | 19 |
| partner | 11 |
| persistent | 18 |
| primary child-care provider | 19 |
| role model | 11 |
| second | 7 |
| set ... priorities | 12 |
| similarly | 7 |
| since | 16 |
| stable | 11 |
| such as | 7 |
| then | 7 |
| therefore | 3 |
| thus | 7 |
| to sum up | 7 |
| transition | 18 |
| unless | 16 |
| until | 16 |
| whereas | 16 |
| whether | 16 |
| while | 16 |

## Chapter 2

| | |
|---|---|
| approach to | 45 |
| capture | 37 |
| caught | 37 |
| contaminated | 29 |
| contemporary | 45 |
| depict | 37 |
| device | 29 |
| display | 36 |
| distributing | 30 |
| exhibition | 36 |
| explicit | 45 |
| fashion | 30 |

| hue | 37 |
| images | 36 |
| immortalize | 36 |
| inconsistent | 45 |
| inevitable | 46 |
| judiciously | 29 |
| machine | 29 |
| model | 30 |
| modifying | 45 |
| mount | 36 |
| much needed | 29 |
| necessary | 32 |
| output | 29 |
| paint | 36 |
| pigment | 37 |
| portray | 36 |
| prototype | 29 |
| record | 37 |
| render | 37 |
| replicate | 30 |
| show | 36 |
| subject | 36 |
| subject matter | 36 |
| test | 30 |
| theme | 36 |
| transform | 46 |
| trial | 29 |
| uniformity | 45 |
| yield | 32 |

### Chapter 3

| agricultural | 57 |
| annually | 61 |
| approximately | 55 |
| assessment | 55 |
| biological | 61 |

| biologist | 56 |
| celestial | 55 |
| coastal | 56 |
| concentrations | 56 |
| conditioner | 56 |
| construction | 56 |
| decrease | 57 |
| depression | 68 |
| dramatic | 56 |
| elevation | 56 |
| encounter | 67 |
| encounter | 68 |
| extinction | 57 |
| extraction | 57 |
| geological | 56 |
| geophysical | 61 |
| glacial | 55 |
| global | 55 |
| historic | 56 |
| hydro- meteorological | 61 |
| immediately | 56 |
| indigenous | 56 |
| industrialization | 56 |
| inscriptions | 56 |
| interdependent | 57 |
| intergovernmental | 55 |
| marginal | 57 |
| microscopic | 56 |
| multinational | 55 |
| nonmigratory | 56 |
| orientation | 55 |
| recently | 55 |
| scientist | 57 |
| seek | 68 |
| series | 68 |

| shift | 55 |
| subsistence | 57 |
| technological | 61 |
| triggered | 67 |
| typically | 55 |
| uncertain | 55 |
| viable | 57 |
| vulnerability | 56 |
| vulnerable | 57 |

## Chapter 4

| adjusting | 82 |
| advocate | 77 |
| alternative | 86 |
| ambiguous | 76 |
| appropriate | 87 |
| assure | 82 |
| check | 77 |
| considerable | 77 |
| conventional | 87 |
| discretion | 77 |
| draw attention | 77 |
| emerging | 87 |
| establish | 87 |
| excluded | 82 |
| exploit | 77 |
| flee | 76 |
| framework | 83 |
| grant | 76 |
| guidelines | 87 |
| impact | 77 |
| minor | 87 |
| priority | 83 |
| resolution | 82 |
| restoration | 83 |
| secure | 82 |

| snap decision | 77 |
| so-called | 86 |
| solely | 77 |
| take up | 77 |
| vary | 77 |
| violation | 76 |
| win a case | 77 |

## Chapter 5

| accept | 100 |
| accommodating | 114 |
| adapt | 100 |
| adjust | 99 |
| adjustment | 99 |
| anxiety | 100 |
| consume | 107 |
| contribution | 107 |
| conventions | 108 |
| cool | 99 |
| dysfunctional | 100 |
| emerge | 99 |
| encounter | 99 |
| estrangement | 99 |
| euphoria | 99 |
| excited | 99 |
| frustration | 99 |
| functional | 100 |
| happiness | 99 |
| identity | 114 |
| illustrate | 107 |
| impact | 99 |
| indecision | 99 |
| interpretation | 107 |
| invariably | 114 |
| misinterpreted | 107 |
| motivation | 107 |

| | |
|---|---|
| perspective | 107 |
| process | 99 |
| pursuing | 114 |
| recovery | 100 |
| resentment | 99 |
| respond | 99 |
| sector | 113 |
| transforming | 114 |
| undergo | 99 |
| unpredictability | 113 |
| withdraw | 100 |

## Chapter 6

| | |
|---|---|
| achieve the goal | 123 |
| assess | 129 |
| beneficial | 129 |
| bulk up | 123 |
| cadaver | 136 |
| colleague | 130 |
| consistent with | 129 |
| cricothyroidotomy | 136 |
| debate | 129 |
| do drugs | 123 |
| document | 130 |
| establish | 130 |
| evolve | 135 |
| implicitly | 136 |
| inherently | 135 |
| insufficiently | 135 |
| keep in shape | 123 |
| perception | 130 |
| plays to win | 123 |
| protocol | 135 |
| rigid | 135 |
| rigor mortis | 135 |
| surreptitiously | 136 |

| | |
|---|---|
| test one's abilities | 123 |
| trachea | 136 |
| via | 136 |
| virtual | 136 |
| work out | 123 |

## Chapter 7

| | |
|---|---|
| abstract | 153 |
| approach | 162 |
| authority | 156 |
| bounce around | 156 |
| challenged | 161 |
| compensate | 148 |
| constant | 161 |
| diverse | 155 |
| exposed to | 162 |
| find oneself | 156 |
| follow suit | 154 |
| have a hand in | 156 |
| income | 148 |
| innovative | 148 |
| mediated | 156 |
| minimal | 162 |
| on the tip of one's tongue | 156 |
| orientation | 153 |
| precede | 148 |
| prime | 148 |
| priorities | 154 |
| ring true | 156 |
| serve up | 156 |
| stand up for | 153 |
| straightforward | 153 |
| take for granted | 153 |
| tell off | 153 |
| unifying | 155 |

## Chapter 8

| | |
|---|---|
| approach | 181 |
| contend | 187 |
| detect | 181 |
| dynamic | 174 |
| ephemeral | 175 |
| equip | 182 |
| examine | 187 |
| expose | 174 |
| facilitate | 174 |
| get into trouble | 175 |
| identify | 182 |
| learn the hard way | 174 |
| maintain | 180 |
| phenomenon | 172 |
| posit | 187 |
| post online | 174 |
| potential | 172 |
| prospects | 174 |
| require | 180 |
| revealing | 174 |
| see in person | 172 |
| stay in touch | 172 |
| take notice | 174 |